More Cotton, Cornbread, and Conversations

MERCER
UNIVERSITY PRESS

Endowed by
TOM WATSON BROWN
and
THE WATSON-BROWN FOUNDATION, INC.

More Cotton, Cornbread, and Conversations

50 New Adventures in Central Georgia

Suzanne Lawler

MERCER UNIVERSITY PRESS | MACON, GEORGIA | 2007

ISBN 978-0-88146-049-0
MUP/P362

© 2007 Mercer University Press
1400 Coleman Avenue
Macon, Georgia 31207
All rights reserved

First Edition.

Book design by Burt & Burt Studio.

All photography by Suzanne Lawler unless otherwise indicated.

∞The paper used in this publication meets the minimum requirements
of American National Standard for Information Sciences—Permanence
of Paper for Printed Library Materials, ANSI Z39.48-1992.

Library of Congress Cataloging-in-Publication Data

Lawler, Suzanne, 1968–
Cotton, cornbread, and conversations:
50 adventures in central Georgia / Suzanne Lawler.
p. cm.
Includes index.
ISBN 978-0-88146-049-0 (pbk.: alk. paper)
1. Georgia—Description and travel—Anecdotes.
2. Georgia—History, Local—Anecdotes.
3. Georgia—Biography—Anecdotes. I. Title.

F286.6.L39 2004
917.5'804043—dc22

2004002830

Festivals and Fun

Stores, Tours, and More

People

This year a dog came into my life. His name is Salty and I must admit, on mornings and afternoons when maybe I should have been pounding the keyboard a bit more, I found myself pounding the pavement, romping around with the frisky puppy. But on those walks that started out as ten-minute jaunts and now last for an hour or so, the thought occurred to me that if dogs could read this book it could become a bestseller because the essence of what I hope you (the humans) get out of the book is something canines know all about: the love of the trip and the thrill of discovering new things.

I had so much fun meeting folks and talking to people about the first *Cotton, Cornbread, and Conversations*, but what really touched my heart the most is hearing the stories of folks taking the pages along in the car and making a journey of the fifty places in Central Georgia. We really do have so much in this area to explore and experience.

In this book, you'll have to strap yourself in for much of the same type of Adventure. You'll meet a man who bought an old Christmas tree farm just so he would have space for hundreds of hostas for sale. The food at Chef Audrey's restaurant in Warner Robins is outstanding, but she owes a good bit of her success to a contest that began as a road game with her boys when they were growing up—and even Salty got his paws involved in this project. He'll tell you about his favorite place in Macon and the only requirement is that you take along your four-footed best friend.

So have fun, be safe, and tell everyone I said "hi" when you set out on your fifty adventures.

ACKNOWLEDGMENTS

Human beings rarely accomplish their dreams on their own. Just as it takes a village to raise a child, it takes friendship, diligence, and a helpful ear to turn out a book. So I will always be thankful to the following people. Kim Smaha is the best friend I could ever have. She's seen the frustration and the joy of this process and has stood by my side the whole way.

This year I was incredibly fortunate to have a childhood friend come back into my life. You know how it goes with friends after college: folks tend to drift. Jan Ward found her way to Central Georgia and she's gone on quite a few of these adventures giving a mom's opinion with little three-year-old Amy in tow. They've tasted pecan pies from Priester's and picked flowers at the farm in Crawford County, and I'm deeply appreciative of the friendship that picked up right where we left off and the company on the road.

On this book, I had a special scout running down interesting places. I met her through another dear friend, MaryTherese Tebbe. MT's mom is a traveling fool and she frequently emails or writes notes of her curious finds. Thanks to Judi Grabowski and Louise Pacheco.

I am fortunate to have a wonderful publisher knocking out these adventures. And there is nothing better than spending an hour or two chatting with the crew at Mercer Press (Sometimes we even talk about the book…ha ha.). Thanks Marc Jolley, Marsha, Barbara, Kevin, Dana, Jenny, and Niccole.

Thank you to Angie Wright. Just knowing you're a phone call away makes some days a little more manageable.

Thanks to Marie Smaha, Don McGouirk and Miloy Summerall for an extra set of eyes in the editing process.

And last, but not least, thanks to Mom and Dad. I am blessed to have two wonderful parents who are very supportive and understanding, especially when I don't make it home during the writing years.

Finally, thanks to everyone who plunks down the money to buy this book. I hope you travel safely on your adventures!

Farms and Frolicking

Hostas.

Hosta Farm

I don't know why folks say gardeners have a green thumb; I think the love of dirt kind of runs throughout their blood. That's how it is for Andy Glore. The guy loves plants and he just hadn't found his niche, or leaf, in life until one day he paused on the side of the road. "I was on a business trip in North Carolina" he explains, "and I stopped at a nursery."

Then something caught his eye: a hosta plant. "It was a Francis William and I said, 'That's beautiful.' The next year, it came back and I said, 'Hey, I need to get some more of them.'"

And that's exactly what he did. He acquired so many of them he and his wife Denise had to move to a beautiful place in Byron with a cedar house and space that was used as a Christmas tree farm. Now, they have 15 acres and sell the plants to other folks who want to make a plant pit stop.

But you know, if you don't love gardening you may have never heard of a hosta. It's green and leafy and doubles (or sometimes triples) its size every year with very distinct showy stems. Hostas love shade and sit pretty low to the ground. The simplicity of care is one of the things that attracted Andy to hostas. "You just plant them and leave them alone," Andy says.

There is another thing that tickles the guy about his new crop in life. "The funniest thing about hostas is their names," he says. The guy's got a point. There are thousands of registered hosta varieties; Andy's proud to sport seventy of them on his farm and every single name has a connection. For instance, you can pick up a Fire and Ice, which has green leaves with shoots of yellow. When the leaves curl up, they look like flame. Red October has bright red stems, which Andy says is pretty unusual for a hosta. Halcyon shows off traces of blue and Big Daddy gets 3 feet high and spreads out 5 feet across in the yard. I didn't understand the Minutemen variety. Andy says it's the last one to come up every year. I personally thought the guys from the American Revolution had better timing. Andy just shook his head and said, "I have no idea about that one!"

And then Andy wooed me with a Suzanne and its beautiful mix of green and soft yellow leaves. Yup, needless to say that one went home with me!

The plants will run you anywhere from a few bucks all the way up to some serious dollars. "We have a $75.00 William Lachman. You just can't find it," Andy says. You might think that's pretty pricey for a plant but Andy's seen them go higher. "I'm looking for a Green Army Man," Andy explains with longing in his eyes. "It's a giant. I saw one on eBay for four to five hundred dollars."

He didn't spend the money; he does have his wife to keep him in check. Although Denise, who also loves plants, has had to make some concessions. "It started out his thing; then it grew on me," she says with a smile.

And the place has a mascot. Emma is a tiny rat terrier who will rush out to greet you and accompany you through her greens. She's a might territorial about the land. "This is her garden. She chases chipmunks, and every now and then, drinks water from the pots," Denise says.

Emma's got her work cut out for her. In 2004, Andy's first year, he sold about 500 plants. The next year he quadrupled his sales. He's not sure how big he'll get, but there's one thing that does sit solid in his mind. "I can't remember gardening before Hostas!"

Address: 2060 Newell Road, Byron, Georgia

Directions: The farm is actually in Byron, but you're going to take I-75 heading south from Macon. Take the Warner Robins exit (146) and hang a right. Go straight across Highway 49. Highway 49 turns into Newell Road. Go 2 miles farther and the farm will be on your left. It's the second to the last house on Newell Road. From the interstate, it's just a little over 5 miles.

Hours: By appointment—just give them a call. But don't worry. Andy says that as they get bigger they will set hours.

Phone: (478) 956-0922

Cost: Plants range from $3.50 to $75.00 each.

Extras: It's best to hit this place in the springtime. Andy divides all of his plants, but once their gone you've got to wait until next year.

Rose Lane and Arlinda work on a recipe.

Rose Lane at the Bullard House.

Charlane Plantation

The story of Charlane Plantation is quirky. "I challenged him that he had to make his name synonymous with here, living with me in my little world," explains Rose Lane Leavell, wife of Chuck Leavell, "and doggone if he didn't do it."

Rose Lane Leavell is married to arguably one of the best piano players in the land. Chuck Leavell has a place in the Georgia Music Hall of Fame and for the last twenty years or so he's tickled the ivory for a band you might of heard of—the Rolling Stones.

But Rose and Chuck have woven a patchwork of family, nature, and music and it resides at Charlane Plantation. This 2200 acres of land features pine forests, flocks of quail, and some pretty cushy human accommodations. But I'm getting ahead of myself. Let's start from the beginning.

Rose Lane met Chuck when she worked for Capricorn records in Macon.

"Chuck was musically inclined since birth," she boasts. "In 1967, he joined the house band at the studios."

The house band gig led to a job with the Allman Brothers, but the guys split up after a few years. In the 70s, Chuck was still doing the music thing, but he was quite content to play the role of Mr. Mom for their daughter Amy. "I did worry about him when I came home one day and he had made a strawberry shortcake; it was good but I thought, *Oh, my God, this guy is bored*." The stylish matriarch of the family had a good career going running a clothing store called Cornucopia. But life was about to change for these two.

In 1981, Rose Lane's grandmother passed away, but she passed the family farm, Charlane Plantation, to her granddaughter, so the small family moved. Afterwards Rose Lane got pregnant with their second child Ashley and then one day the phone rang.

"The Rolling Stones called out of the blue," says Rose Lane. They had heard about Chuck's talent on the keyboard, but ironically the musical guy was about to chuck all his instruments. "He was into farming, but I told him to give the Stones a call back," she reminisces. Six months later he had a job and a long destiny of touring from city to city. "Me and my Mom birthed Ashley in the hospital parking lot. We overnighted him the pictures to Madrid." Through music, Chuck found a rebirth of something he loved… but he never lost the passion for farming and the land. Chuck would even go on to win Georgia Tree Farmer of the Year in 1999. You might say both lifestyles complemented each other.

Rose Lane and Chuck bought a few hundred acres adjacent to Charlane Plantation. One day they were wandering through the woods and found a true jewel among the trees—well, a rundown jewel but still a jewel. "It was an 1835 farmhouse with rotted porches and a tree growing right up through the middle," Rose mentions. Turns out that dilapidated piece of property was originally the Bullard House (named after the riverboat captain who owned it years ago). Rose Lane and Chuck fixed it up to a beautiful cabin. As for that old tree that was growing up in the middle, now pieces of it adorn headboards in one of the rooms and part of the stump is laid into the gorgeous bar in the back of another lodge that sits directly across the way. The former Bullard House now looks like a hunting lodge with rustic accommodations: an antler door handle and floor-to-ceiling lumber milled on the plantation. You won't find any phoness, but the lodges do have cable television and rocking chairs sit on the front porch overlooking tubs of blooming flowers on the grounds.

The Bullard lodge also has a pool table—and a scrumptious menu. "The number one reason people come is the food; hunting is secondary." Rose Lane loves to cook, and guys out hunting tend to like three squares a day. So on any given occasion you might find fried quail with sweet potato soufflé on the supper menu, and fresh local bacon is fried up in the morning and the condiments get whipped up right in the kitchen.

The day I stopped by, Rose Lane and her lead cooking partner, Arlinda Height, were trying to iron out the perfect recipe for mint jelly. Rose Lane had a plan: "I know what I want and she helps me get it," she explains. "I want it sweet and sour and *very* minty." Arlinda started by walking out on the front porch and yanking vines of fresh mint out of the garden. (In fact, most of the veggies and herbs come out of the garden.) But Arlinda thinks that it's the meatier cuisine that gets some folks to start drooling. "Our ribs are to die for; it's our own special rub!" she says with a smile.

Hunters have a good time. It's hard not to with stocked woods, four horses, and a kennel full of twenty feisty dogs to help out on the adventure. Well, actually make that nineteen feisty dogs. "See that one on the end. Yup, we've got one useless French hunting dog," Rose says with a smile. He's probably a lover not a fighter.

If romance is more your style, don't rule out Charlane Plantation. The tall pines do provide a shady quiet getaway for a quick vacation. Rose Lane showed me a beautiful water garden, nature trails, and places for folks to just get away and relax.

In 2005, Chuck and Rose Lane headed out for another Rolling Stones tour—those guys will probably keep playing into the twenty-second century —but if the big guy is in town don't be surprised if he sits down at the piano to play a tune. After all, for this family that's played their way around the world, nothing beats a good meal at home and special times at Charlane Plantation.

Phone: (478) 945-3939 (You'll usually get a recording, but don't worry. Someone will call you back.)

Websites: charlaneplantation.com. Also, check out chuckleavell.com and rosieworld.com.

Extras: You've got to call first to stop by. They don't give private tours. They do book weddings retreats and conferences all year. Quail season runs October through March.

An agave plant sits in the sun.

Murali says hello to the fish.

Lockerly Arboretum

Nestled in a Milledgeville neighborhood is one of the best and most colorful secrets in town—Lockerly Arboretum, a sprawling 50 acres of unusual greenery and fun.

Murali Thirumal has spent eighteen years finding, nurturing, and growing the plants. He runs the place and heads up the small staff. And for this spiritual man from Sri Lanka, the arboretum is a second home and a way of life. "It does everything life needs to do for one. It's therapy, it's spiritual, and it's a challenge. It's a place that gives us humility to work in."

When you walk or drive around the grounds, it's easy to understand where Murali is coming from, especially if you take the time to sit down by the pond. There is a wooden bench that looks out over the serene area. Even in the Georgia heat, you'll want to sit down and just take in the water lilies, conifers, and everything else that makes up this collection. It felt like a kind of heaven.

But with all of that being said there is a whimsical side to the garden, and that's how I met Gilbert and Mary Brust, who just stopped by for a visit. These two came down from Massachusetts and just picked Dublin out on the map as their new home. Gilbert quickly informed me of their green thumb pecking order. "She's the gardener; my job is the lawn," he says with pride.

The gardener and the lawn boy both stopped in their tracks when they saw the century plant, otherwise known as Agave. It looks like something that came right out of the *Little Shop of Horrors*; maybe Mary explained it best when she saw it. "Oh, my goodness, what is that? I hope it doesn't attack us," she says.

The cactus-like plant stands over 8 feet tall, and its bluish silver limbs look more like spiky hair flowing out of a Medusa head. But it is completely harmless and actually once—just once in its lifetime—it throws out a flower. "Tequila is made from it in Mexico, and once it throws out a flower it is done," explains Murali, "but contrary to its name it doesn't take a century!" "It's neat but I wouldn't want it in my yard," Mary decides.

Something else you'll probably never see in the Brusts' landscape plan is the stinky plant. When these things bloom they usually make the news, and you'll see folks walking by holding their noses. Murali says they get one to stink up the place (or at least the greenhouse) every spring. "The bulb is 30–40 pounds. It puts out a single bloom that got to 7 feet last year."

Well, as you can tell by the two previous examples these guys search the globe for unusual plants. And you can read up on every leaf: the plants, trees, and shrubbery all come with tags that include the common, family scientific name, and their origin.

The founding of the arboretum itself is all thanks to a man by the name of Edward J. Grassman. He liked the area and worked hard to get the local kaolin industry off the ground. He also had a vision for the grounds surrounding Lockerly Hall, which is an antebellum mansion that sits on the property. In front of the massive house is a long pool that is home to dozens of beautiful Koi and goldfish. "We call them pigs because when they see you they go into a feeding frenzy," Murali explains. It's pretty entertaining, so don't miss those colorful clowns, but make sure you also check out the various collections antique roses, tropicals, and bonsais.

When it's all said and done it may give you some of the humility that the staff feels fortunate to feel every day working in such a beautiful atmosphere.

Address: 1534 Irwinton Road (Highway 441), Milledgeville, Georgia

Directions: From Macon, take Highway 49 toward Milledgeville. Take a right on the bypass onto Highway 441. Take your next left on Allen Memorial Drive. Go to the stop sign and take a left. You'll see the sign for the Arboretum on your right.

Hours: Monday through Saturday, call or check the website for seasonal hours. Murali and his crew take Sundays off.

Phone: (478) 452-2112

Website: www.lockerlyarboretum.org

Prices: Here's the great part: it's free!

Extras: You cannot buy or take cuttings from any of the plants at the arboretum, but they do have an annual plant sale that offers some unusual stuff. To see Lockerly Hall, you've got to book tours through the Milledgeville convention and visitors bureau. Those trips run on Mondays and Wednesdays. For more information you can call (478) 452-4687.

This peach is ready to eat!

Peggy Jerles.

Big Six Peach and Pecan Farm

Peggy Jerles fondly remembers her elementary school days. It's not hard since the family business sits nestled in the old school house in Zenith, Georgia.

Five generations back, Peggy's Great Grandfather Moses Winlock Pearson began Big Six Farms and named his business after his six sons. In those days, the schoolhouse never sat too far away from the fields, and Peggy attended class through fifth grade with about sixty other kids. In 1950, the old school house closed and the Jerles purchased the building and the land. At first, they just used it as a shed to dry pecans…and the kids found some creative recreation inside the walls. "We would come up here and skate," Peggy says with a twinkle in her eye.

Nowadays, Peggy comments, impromptu class reunions happen. "People come by and say I went to school here." Those people see the same hardwood floors lining the old building, but what happens inside on a daily basis is a lot different.

From the middle of May to the beginning of August, workers sort, pack, and polish thousands of pounds of Pearson peaches. Big Six sports 1500 acres of the top Georgia fruit and 1500 acres of pecans.

When you walk in the door, you're greeted by the inner workings of the entire operation as peaches go spiraling down the line. You can climb up on the catwalk to get a birds-eye view of the place. In this bright airy atmosphere, fresh bouquets of zinnias perch on little tables, fresh produce like eggplant, watermelon, and squash sit at attention, and a big icy peach ice cream machine swirls out a summer treat. In 2005, a half-bushel of peaches with the morning dew still sparkling on the skin would run you nine bucks. And if you're a might more partic- ular about your fruit, just bring your own container and you can pick the peaches right off the line.

If Peggy isn't there to chat, you can find her picture on the back wall. It's a short pictorial 8x10 black and white history of how things have evolved through the years. "Back then we didn't have I-75. Everybody came down 341," she explains, "so we had little stands and we sold peaches. If you had two boxes and a board, you were in busi- ness."

Today, the majority of traffic travels I-75, peaches come in corru- gated boxes as opposed to the old crates, and it's harder to put two boards together and have a business. Six growers in the state do 95 percent of the peach business, and since Big Six stands as one of those proud growers, its name still rings true. But the connections don't stop there. You see, Peggy is the oldest of three siblings; they are all married and so there are still six people running the place.

Mary Pearson married one of Peggy's brothers, and has the respon- sibility of running Pearson Farm. If you can't make it out to the Big Six packing shed, you can stop by this wonderful little store to get everything you need. In season, you can buy peaches. All year round they have various pecans, some toasted, some salted, and some with a decadent chocolate covering. As a matter of fact, Martha Stewart has even given these guys a call to get an order of Elliott pecans. Peggy says cooks love them because they've got a lot of oil to them. "Just strike a match to these pecans and they'll just flame up," she says. So I asked her how many times she tried the little pyro trick. "Just once," she admits.

You'd better close this book right here if you have a sweet tooth because what these folks whip up will have you making a beeline for the place. When you stop by, order up a slice of peach cake. They also make whipping cream pound cakes and pecan buttermilk and choco- late pies. A second peach ice cream machine competes with its cousin out at the shed. Mary says each place has its own little unique flavor. That may be true, but Big Six and Pearson Farms run hand in hand supplying folks with some of the best peaches and pecans in the area, and that's a lesson that's hard to forget.

Big Six Farm

Directions: From Macon, go south on I-75 to the Byron exit (149). Take a right off the ramp heading towards Fort Valley. Ten miles down the road you'll see signs to get on the Bypass and follow the signs to the farm (about ten minutes away).

Hours: Peach season runs from May to about the beginning of August. You can stop in between nine to five to buy peaches and get a cup of ice cream.

Extras: When it comes to peach-packing sheds in the summertime, you may also want to visit Dickey's in Musella, Wainwright's in Reynolds, and Lane Packing featured in the original *Cotton, Cornbread, and Conversations.*

Pearson Farms

Address: 11022 Highway 341, Fort Valley, Georgia

Directions:. Pearson Farms is on Highway 341 just a few miles from Perry. If you're going by the interstate from Macon, take exit 136. Turn right. Go 3.5 miles and the store will be on the left.

Hours: June–December, 10:00 A.M.–5:00 P.M. During the holidays and Peach season they are open on Saturdays. You can shop here all year. Fresh peaches are in season mid-June to mid-August, and Vidalia onions are in from May to July. Pecans are year round as are gift baskets.

Phone: (478) 827-0750; 888-423-7374

Website: www.pearsonfarm.com

Naomi and Bennie.

Naomi picks some great basil.

Davis Farms

You might figure Yankees know a thing or two about Bronx Bomber baseball, snowstorms, and Sicilian pizza, but Southern produce? Come on that's all ours right? Well, Naomi Davis is nurturing some of the best 'maters, cukes, and watermelons out of the ground every summer.

And how it all got started at the Davis Farm in Crawford County is quite a story. "I was raised in the Bronx and moved down here in 2000," she says. The story didn't start out cheery. Naomi's husband had cancer, and they moved to Warner Robins because he had a sister in the area also fighting cancer. The disease proved to be deadly for both members of the family. He passed and then the devastation of September 11 struck. Naomi, who ran an employment agency, had a lot of friends that didn't make it out of the towers, and she just couldn't go back.

So she sold jewelry at Smiley's Flea Market. She and a friend took a liking to a sweet guy named Mack who sold produce in a nearby booth. "He was really nice and on Sundays he would give us leftover watermelon, but one day Mack didn't show up," she explains. After a couple of weeks of not seeing her friend, another man by the name of Bennie had the absolute audacity to move in on the booth and start selling produce. "I'm a typical New Yorker, so I told him, 'Hey, that's Mack's space' and I remember the very first words he said to me: 'Sugar, Mack's in the hospital and I'm his brother,'" she says with a twinkle in her eye.

Now don't worry. Mack made it out of the hospital, and on Valentine's Day 2003, the unlikely couple Bennie and Naomi made it to the altar. I say unlikely because Bennie is a big strapping farmer type who likes to wear overalls. His family has acres and acres of land they used for hog farming, and Naomi, well, she spent her life in the fast lane up north, but the two did quickly find some common ground.

"We laugh about it all the time," she says. "We got back from our honeymoon and one day I was reading the *Farmers Bulletin*. There was a workshop on Team Agriculture and I was interested. Bennie said, 'Honey, I farmed before,' but I said 'Yes, but I haven't, so lets go!'" So the New Yorker dragged the farmer back out on the land to develop Davis Farms round two.

You can stop by anytime for fresh produce but the couple wants to really develop community farming. That's where folks pay a certain amount of money each week and come by and get bags of whatever's in season.

The couple farm organically, meaning they don't use any pesticides or insecticides not approved by the USDA, and now the woman from New York speaks like a regular farming gal connected to the land. "Marigolds attract good insects, and nematodes help with Japanese beetles," she says. But for all that know-how, Naomi admits that not all of this comes naturally. "I still walk out with clippers and nothing to harvest with," she says, laughing.

The Davises harvest bunches of crops herbs, strawberries, and collards just to name a few. But in the summertime, folks make a beeline to the property for one thing. "Tomatoes, tomatoes, tomatoes. I could never plant enough," she says. "They don't want them to taste like cardboard; they want homegrown."

Well, along with those homegrown tomatoes is a woman who now has a different state and culture to claim as her own. And Middle Georgians are fortunate to have a place that can fill their fridges with homegrown fruits and vegetables.

Address: 701 Hortman Mill Road, Roberta, Georgia

Directions: Hortman Mill Road is right behind the old Crawford County Courthouse. The farm is just a few miles up the road going south. If you get to Davis Tire, you've gone too far.

Hours: Call for appointment.

Phone: (478) 836-4564

Extras: They sell corn, watermelon, peppers, collards, snap beans, squash, potatoes, onions, mustard, and herbs. If you bring a fishing pole, you can also land fresh catfish from the Davis's pond. If you want to keep them, it will run you a buck or two a pound and she knows there are some whoppers that live on the property.

My little friend Amy couldn't resist picking some flowers.

Paul and Delise.

Delise loves to let kids check out the chickens.

Pineola Farms

Rarely do history buffs get to surround themselves with the past like Paul and Delise Knight do every day. The Knights own a farm that's stood in Peach County for more than 140 years, and they can't wait to share their land and its history and stories.

Now, the Knights always loved antiques, but little did they know that one day they would wake up in one every morning. "We moved out here in 1997," Paul recalls. Delise adds, "We saw the home on a Sunday morning, came in, walked around, and fell in love. By Wednesday afternoon, we had a house that we didn't know we were going to buy."

The impromptu purchase moved the couple out of Macon and onto 12 acres of pecan-tree-lined renowned land. Stephen Bassett and his kin originally owned the property. Bassett worked as a minister and built the dog-trot-style house in 1865. "A dog-trot frame means the front door and back door are a mirror image with a hall running through the center," Delise explains.

The house isn't huge, but it's chock full of things from the past, which mix with warm memories from the present. "Nothing came with the house, but lot of things came back to the house," says Delise. You'll see black-and-white photos from the Bassett family sitting next to snapshots of Paul and Delise's numerous nieces and nephew's playing outside. The rooms are semi-formal. Original Czechoslovakian crystal chandeliers hang from the ceiling and an old worn weather barometer adorns the coffee table. The kitchen is big, yellow, and very inviting and a long wooden table stretches out in the dining room. Big farm baskets and buggy chairs hang from the ceiling, and you get the idea this room gets some use. Delise says she does spend a good bit of time in the galley, which differs from her life a few years back. "We lived in North Macon. If I wanted food, I just got in the car. Out here you have to cook and I've learned."

For all the finery inside the house, there is an open invitation not to treat this place like a museum. "This is a lived-in house. Nothing is not touchable. In fact, the kids have contests on who can jump higher on the beds," Delise says with a big smile on her face.

The kids and the adults can also romp around outside…especially when it's festival time. Paul and Delise like to show folks some of the ways of the past on the property. So during the fall festival, you'll find Paul's Dad hunkered down on a flatbed tinkering with the other old timers on simple gasoline engines. And alongside the boiled peanuts and rows of pansies for sale, you may spy a simple red steel contraption, one I simply had to ask about. "It lets kids shell corn and grind corn into meal," Paul explains as he started cranking. "We want to show them corn doesn't just come from the grocery store, and actually this is a fancy hand crank because the cob spits out the side!" Along with the corn, a house full of chickens provides fresh eggs for the couple. You get the feeling Delise sees these fancy feathered fowl as friends as she holds them out for kids to pet and touch. "Well, they are designer chickens with britches and pantaloons," she explains.

And if you love to carve a pumpkin when the weather cools down, these guys have quite a selection to take home with you. All along the front lawn, giant orange gourds stand watch on the grounds. You can hear the excitement as kids yell, "Hey, Dad, what about this one?" And I swear the day I visited, every pumpkin had a very long twisty stem—very important in my book. The Knights know a guy at the Atlanta Farmers' Market (also worth a trip if you get the chance) that hooks them up with some unusual stuff like bluish gray pumpkins or the plump muted orange ones that are a bit fancier than most.

It's a lot of fun for this couple that stumbled into their destiny. But maybe Delise puts it best when it comes to owning a piece of the past that's very much alive today: "We don't own this home; we are caretakers of this house in this time in its life."

Directions: From Macon, take 1-75 South to Byron (exit 149). Hang a right off the ramp. Go 9.9 miles and take a right on the bypass onto the Highway 49 connector. It's just past the golf course. At the first crossroads, take a right onto Taylor's Mill Road. The house is a quarter-mile down the road on the left. When it's festival time, Paul and Delise have signs up to guide you through.

Website: www.pineola.com

Phone: (478) 827-0894

Prices: If you want to book a luncheon wedding or just an afternoon tour, you must call for reservations. The charge for a historical tour through the house and the land will run you $6.00. Luncheons are $17.00 per person and they include tasty dishes like puff pastries and chocolate trifles. And, yes, the eggs come straight from the coop.

Extras: Delise and Paul open the farm three times a year for wonderful events. There is a fall festival complete with hayrides and a pumpkin patch. The first Saturday in December is their Christmas celebration during which you can also pick up your holiday tree. The spring event occurs the first weekend in May. This is more for gardeners. You'll find plenty of plants to pick through to fill your gardens for the season.

Chickens like bread.

Sissy Hair showing off some beautiful plants.

Antique pitcher for sale.

Easy Living
Garden Center
and Antique Store

Folks that have green thumbs tend to inherit the talent and Leah Hair is no different. The owner of the Easy Living Garden Center grew up on a farm in Dooley County. She enjoyed the simple life of growing up in the country, but she also endured the hardships of what life can throw at a family. "'Bout the time I got to the fourth grade my Daddy had emphysema. He had to stop working, so my Mama took in sewing," she says.

Her mom instilled a strong work ethic in Leah, but her mom also taught her daughter to find pleasure in the simple things in life. "She did have flowers. I didn't know the names of them, but I helped her with them."

Early on Leah learned the importance of earning a living: she and her brother started a lawn-mowing business and when she grew up she began working with heavy machinery at the Weyhauser plant. "I worked in the wood yard unloading trucks and turning trees into little bitty chips," she explains.

Leah eventually came into contact with a good many contractors, guys that didn't know too much about flowers. "There was a shortage of folks who knew anything about plants," she says. "Next thing I know I was doing full-scale landscaping. I liked it so much I put in a nursery."

It's more than a nursery, it's a wonderful adventure for anyone who loves unusual things. A little cottage house is surrounded by acres of land full of green plants, tall trees, and eye-popping pottery. Tons of critters and knickknacks for the yard also heavily dot the landscape. You'll find everything from angels and anchors to frogs and faces, along with terra cotta and concrete squirrels nestled in among the annuals and perennials.

Sissy Hair is Leah's niece. She says she can't help working in the family business: "It's in my blood."

Sissy showed off some of the pottery, which can be any color of the rainbow and any shape you could dream could hold a plant. "The purple and pink is new. You can only go with a select color of flower when you plant in them, that's for sure," she says.

I couldn't resist taking home a purple pot. I figured some mint would do quite nicely inside. Sissy says some of their pieces are high-end out of England, but there's plenty of stuff that's more affordable, too.

Even though I originally found this place because I can't resist stopping in at a nursery, there is a whole other side to the business: antiques. Leah's had them since she opened up.

"I've been collecting for so many years every closet was full and the attic was full," she says with a chuckle. "They were just sitting there and nobody could see them and if you're going to collect you gotta get rid of some to keep collecting."

So inside the cottage, with sunshine bouncing off the hardwood floors, you'll find Depression glass, pottery from Roseville, some Coca Cola memorabilia, and old photographs. She also carries some select furniture and a wall full of University of Georgia stuff just to keep the bulldogs happy. Hanging down from the rafters are two colonial doors that came out of an old dime store, and although folks ask, the doors are one of the few things that aren't for sale.

The family's even converting an old feed-and-seed building out back into an antique mall and that's where I found one of their hot sellers, an item that would only take off in the South:

iron, tractor-seat bar stools. Yup, nothing like feeling that you're in the field when you sit down for a cocktail, but Leah says they can't keep them in stock. The small ones will run you $48.00, while the tall boys ring up at $69.00.

Sissy says the antiques just give her aunt an outlet to do what she loves. "She is a big eBayer. Her and my Uncle Glenn love estate sales and also go hunting at Smiley's [a local flea market]."

I asked Leah if she's proud of how things turned out for the farm girl from humble beginnings, and she told me she's bewildered by the whole thing. "I'm amazed at how big it's become. I wasn't expecting it to grow like it has," she says.

But the woman who may be hauling concrete rocks or unloading heavy pottery has found that devoting all her time to this family endeavor has come with an occupational challenge. "I don't get to plant my own plants anymore," she says. But she is planting the seeds for thousands of other gardeners to enjoy one of the things her mom tended to when life got tough: blooming beautiful flowers.

Directions: Take I-75 South from Macon. Turn left off exit 138 onto Thompson Road, and the nursery will be a few miles up the road on your left. 400 North Perry Parkway.

Hours: Summer, 9:00 A.M.–6:00 P.M.; winter, 9:00 A.M. –5:00 P.M.; March through Father's Day, 1:00 P.M.–6:00 P.M. on Sundays

Phone: (478) 987-8910

Extras: They also have an enormous Christmas showroom to celebrate the holiday, and the team also does landscaping work. And if you really just need something insanely unique in your yard, I did see an outhouse for sale; it will run you $300.

Helen Wilder holds up giant home grown cabbage.

Homemade slices of cake for sale.

Downtown Byron Market

In a world where we get most of our produce from grocery stores and super centers, it's good to enjoy something fresh from the farm. Every Saturday morning from April to September, about a dozen vendors line up at the old Byron schoolhouse parking lot ready for business. Here you'll find everything from homegrown hydrangeas to unbelievable birdhouses. All kinds of plants stand ready to go while the bumper crop of summer veggies arrive in the summertime.

When I walked up to Helen Wilder, her table looked bare yet the woman still sat in her lawn chair by the side of a truck. Helen told me she had sold out of her giant cabbage running two bucks a head so she sent her husband home to Fort Valley to quickly cut some more! "One lady bought one and she didn't even like cabbage," Helen explains, "but she said it was so pretty she was going to carry it to her family reunion."

The Mennonite table is pretty popular especially if you have a sweet tooth. The ladies lay out every kind of cake imaginable as well as lemon cheese treats. They also sell cookies, fresh bread, and chess bar squares.

Linda Dupree has set up shop every summer for three years now. At her booth in the corner under the shade of a big pecan tree, you'll find Red Lobster, Chick Fil-A, and McDonald's cups all holding her healthy looking tomato plants. There's a reason for the Styrofoam, everything at this market has got to be homemade or homegrown. So folks get creative in their packaging. "The big cups run $1.25 and the smaller ones go for seventy-five cents," she says. "Most people figure even if they kill them, they're not out much money." Killing your new purchase is out of the question if you quiz Linda when you make your purchase. Linda loves to give out the advice along with your change. "Just dig a trench, strip it down, and you should only see the top of the tomato plant," she told a woman as she took home a couple of the plants.

Linda sells angel trumpets, which she claims the deer don't like too much, and an unusual plant called lavender cotton that smells fresh like greenery you pulled right out of the dryer! She loves the plants but she really likes the people that stop by every weekend. "I love it, I just love to talk plants and gardening," she says.

And that's the magic of this place. "Half of the people shop here for the relationships," Joan Hayes explains with a smile on her face.

Joan should know, she's spearheaded this project. A person on the Byron Hometown Board gave her the idea after they visited a similar place up in West Virginia. Joan liked the way it sounded and set out to work. Her family wound up tagging along for all of the groundwork. "It was hard finding farmers, and every day after school I would say to the kids, 'Come on, we're going to the country,'" she recalls.

Joan harvested quite a lineup of folks who love the land and a few artists to boot. Then she secured things with the city and set up a thirty-year lease to ensure the success of the little market. "It's like coming home," she says. "Some people just come for the social aspect. They walk around and talk. These people are really family by the end of the season."

As she walks around with her daughter darting from one area to another, Joan does feel a sense of accomplishment. "The proudest moment came when Hawkinsville called me and said, 'We want to do it,'" she says. "But it doesn't work in every city. It takes community support to make it happen."

By the way, Helen's husband did make it back with some of that popular cabbage, and it was bigger than anything I had ever seen. So do support the Byron market. You might just stop in to scoop up stuff for dinner, but even then you'll leave far richer for the experience.

Directions: From Macon, take I-75 to the Byron exit (149). Take a right off the ramp and go about a mile down the road and turn right.

Hours/Seasons: April 15–September 30, 8:00 A.M.-12:00 P.M.

Phone: (478) 956-5555

Website: www.byronga.com

Extras: Remember this is seasonal stuff, so look for your tomato plants in the spring and look for the corn and green beans come summertime. Many cities do now have their own little weekend markets, so check in your town if you can't make it to Byron. Also, if you're interested in selling plants of produce Joan says it will only cost you $25.00 for the entire season to set up shop.

Linda Dupree bags up more tomatoes.

You can see how big the zinnias get in the garden.

Zinnia's.

Farmer Brown's Market

If you ever pondered the question "Why did the chicken cross the road?" and you're in Macon County, he probably did it to get a better look at the flowers!

Debra and William Brown own and run Farmer Brown's Market, also known as William C. Brown Farms. In Central Georgia, you just can't go wrong stopping at any roadside shed that's selling peaches that came right off the tree that morning. But this place has a little extra surprise for the customers. Besides the juiciest peaches with the fuzz still clinging to the fruit, red ripe tomatoes, and bright yellow squash for sale, you can also scoot across the pavement, armed with a Mason jar and clippers to harvest a bucketful of blooms that come in a bountiful assortment of colors!

Debra's daughter Kim came up with the idea for her Dad to plant more than just veggies. "I just thought the zinnias are so pretty that it would draw people in and people do like to talk about them," she says.

You can't help but go on and on. Each stem runs a dime but they're so big that you would probably plunk down a dollar. "We just plant the zinnias for fun for the customers. We practically give them away," Debra says with a smile. "People can pick after hours over the 3 acres and there is an honor box, but we could just never sell them all." That's because in addition to the 400 acres of peaches the Browns plant 3 acres of the annuals including a large tract of sunflowers. William says folks will stop for different reasons to fill up a jar. "The funniest thing I saw one day is three big burly guys came and got buckets to pick flowers. I said someone's in the doghouse," he recalls.

The blooms make William smile but he and his wife say they're most known for their peaches. The farm's been in the family for decades although like most things the process has evolved. "We used to sell peaches out of a wagon under the pecan tree and put them in brown paper bags and every time it rained we'd have to gather everything up and go get in the truck," Debra says. This female part of this team who goes a mile a minute had bigger plans. "I begged him to build a farmers' market and he turned me loose and it's been a hit."

Now the building still sits under those gorgeous pecan trees in the orchard but now you can watch the rain while sitting on wonderfully worn church pews. Or get out of the sun and shop for farm-themed oil paintings that hang on the wooden walls. "The art adds a little spark to the store with the roosters and flowers," Debra says.

The art and flowers just set the stage for the main ingredient to this family's success: the peaches. "We're known for our Elbertas," Debra says proudly. Elbertas are like the Cadillac variety in the peach industry. "People just go crazy over them."

The Brown's won't ship those peaches because they bruise too easily, but if you're like me and wouldn't know an Elberta from an albatross its okay there's only one thing you really need to appreciate. "We do things the old fashioned way around here," Debra says. "We go into the fields in old peach trailers, pick 'em off the tree, put them in a box, and they go home with the customer usually that same day."

A good many of the peaches get the proud distinction of winding up in the ice cream that's served in the shed along with some other peach goodies. The ice cream has wonderful chunks of the fruit lodging right into your taste buds. Of course, there's a reason it's hard to resist. "It's got about 18 percent butter fat in it," Debra admits. "I gained 10 pounds eating it last summer!" They also serve homemade lemonade and peach crisp, and if you thought the ice cream was decadent, wait till you hear about what Debra calls the peach blossom. "It's like a peach dumpling. You take a peach half and put it in a pastry. Then you put in pure butter spices and juices. We fold it up in a shell, add more butter, and bake it."

John and Alice Baker stop in most afternoons for a cup of ice cream. I sat down with them as they enjoyed their daily ritual. "It's done by hand. You can buy mush from anywhere, but these are good Georgia peaches. We lose the pounds again in the winter," Alice explains.

Don't worry about your weight. It's worth it to take in the whole experience of picking flowers, shopping for peaches and eating some of the stuff Georgia is known for before you go home.

"It's very nostalgic here," Debra thought as she looked around. "This is a gathering place." It's a gathering place where you get to keep enjoying the benefits long after you get home!

Directions: From Macon take I-75 to the Byron exit (149) take a right off the ramp onto Highway 49. You're going to stay on 49 for about a half an hour (Pay attention because you have to stay on 49 and you will make one right at the stop sign in Marshalville.) until you see Farmer Brown's on the side of the road about 11 miles south of Marshalville.

Hours/Seasons: During the peak season, the family opens up at 8:30 in the morning and runs until 6:30 at night, Monday through Saturday. You can stop by Sunday afternoon 1:30–6:30 P.M. Don't forget though, if you want to pick zinnias and the Brown's aren't around, just leave your money in the honor box by the garden. The peaches come in mid-June through mid-August. Now Debra says the Elbertas ripen on the trees about the 15th of July or so and last two to three weeks.

Phone: (478) 472-8767

Extras: A large box of peaches run $13 to $14 dollars, a peck box goes out the door for $7.00. Peach ice cream is $2.00 a cup and one of those massive peach blossom's in a bowl is $3.50. Zinnias are 10 cents a bloom, and if you need a mason jar to carry them home that's only 50 cents.

If you're thinking of growing your own zinnias, here are some good tips. Always choose an area that is well drained and has full sun. Mildew is a big enemy of these plants, so water with a soaker hose or directly on the ground, avoiding the foliage if at all possible. Also, dead heading (removing dead flowers) will keep the blossoms coming!

Debra's Favorite Peach Pie

5–6 cups ripe peaches
1 tbsp. lemon juice
1 cup plain flour, sifted
1/2 tsp. salt
1 egg, beaten
5–6 tbsp. butter, melted
1/2 cup sugar

Peel and slice peaches and sprinkle with 1/2 cup sugar and lemon juice. Set aside. In a separate bowl, mix the other dry ingredients and pour in the beaten egg. Mix well with a fork. Mixture will be sticky. Keep stirring until combined. Pour sweetened slice peaches into a 2-quart casserole that has been sprayed with cooking spray. Sprinkle crumb/egg mixture over top of peaches. Then drizzle melted butter over top. Bake at 350 degrees for 35 to 40 minutes or until slightly browned. Terrific when topped with ice cream.

Restaurants
and Good Eats

Tina tosses the dough.

Ingleside Village Pizza.

Ingleside Pizza

I'm not a big one for ordering pizza from some of the big chains; maybe it's because I'm a bit spoiled by the best place in town for a slice: Ingleside Pizza.

It's not just the food; just walking in can make you smile. It's den-like with dark ceilings and twinkling retro lighting. I mean lamps literally hang down from the ceiling. creating a cozy, comfy place with a black and white checkered floor. Parents can teach their kids the great art of picking songs off a jukebox list…and folks who pride themselves as beer snobs have dozens of brews from around the world to ponder over.

Owner Tina Dixon is the master of her pizza world. She and a former partner started Ingleside Pizza because they didn't like working for someone else. "I'm college educated, but I was working in a restaurant and hating it. The people I was working for couldn't manage or even talk to somebody." A little frustration fueled the entrepreneur so Tina opened up the place on Mother's Day 1992. Her Mom did get free pizza and a coke. "She still gets free pizza," Tina says with a smile.

What you get is a pretty laid-back experience. Folks walk up to a corner cash register and place an order. Waiters bring the piping hot pies out to the table. The younguns—and I must admit folks my age—can pass the time watching professionals spin pizza dough through the air. Or you can get a glob and get creative at your table. If you ask nicely the guys will give you a small mound of dough to play with. "When we first opened, only a couple of us could throw the dough, but the kids would crowd around," explains Tina. A guy by the name of Ben Gause lopped off a piece of the stretchy stuff, gave it to the kids, and a tradition was born. "The kids like making their own pizzas at the table," Tina says, but they do have strict rules on food fights, or throwing the balls of dough. "If that happens, we take the dough back. It's very embarrassing!"

It seems pizza nowadays is as varied as trying to decide what color to wear in the morning. But life is simple at Ingleside; all the usual toppings like pepperoni, sausage, onions, mushroom, and that kind of stuff sit on the menu. All the veggies are fresh and chopped up every single day. I'll let Tina tell you about the sauce. "It's not bogged down with weirdo spices, pretty much tomatoes and basil, and fresh garlic, not fresh from a jar," she says indignantly.

Tina says the Ultimate is their bestseller (which you might imagine has piles of stuff all over the crust), but the most exotic thing on the menu is the white pizza. It's made up of spinach, a heavy dose of white cheese, and enough garlic that you won't need to worry about close contact for a while. Tina did get frisky in the early years, but found out different doesn't always sell. "I had a breakfast pizza. It had ham, bacon, onions, mushroom, and instead of tomatoes sauce, it had eggs. Macon wasn't ready for that, so we substituted white pizza, which Macon loves."

Tina had another surprise coming her way. When she and her partner opened, they figured college kids would love the place as a hangout, but actually the motif appealed to different crowds. "We see a lot of young families, and it's popular with the older generation—that was a surprise. We thought we'd be open until midnight but now we're closed at nine."

Not a bad life for the pizza Mom, and the way Tina sees it she's found a perfect way to please pie lovers in the area. "What I've got works. Why muck it up? There's definitely a niche for good basic pizza!"

Address: 2396 Ingleside Avenue, Macon, Georgia.

Directions: Ingleside Village is located right off Riverside Drive in Macon or going north on I-75, take exit 167, go straight across Riverside Drive down Pierce Avenue until you hit Ingleside Avenue. Take a left onto Ingleside and look ahead and to the right at the next light.

Hours: Tuesday–Friday, 11:00 A.M.–3:00 P.M., 5:00 P.M.–10:00 P.M.; Saturday, 12:00 P.M.–3:00 P.M., 5:00 P.M.–10:00 P.M.; Sunday, 5:00 P.M.–9:00 P.M. Closed Mondays.

Phone: (478) 750-8488

Extras: Tina does have sub sandwiches and a gargantuan salad on the menu. She's even started to serving brownies as dessert. You can order the pizzas by the pie or by the slice, and don't walk away without ordering breadsticks. They're also hand-rolled every day and served in a hearty portion of garlic butter along with a side of tomato sauce for dipping.

Tina just opened a satellite of Ingleside Pizza called 2nd Street Pizza. It's located inside the Capitol Theatre in downtown Macon. The menu is basically the same with the great pizza pies, but they are a little more limited on their slices. The new place is at 382 2nd Street.

Tommy and Tommy.

Tommy, Jr., showin' us what's cooking.

Tucker's Barbeque

Maybe it's a little bit funny looking back now, but one of the best barbeque places in town started because of a case of nerves. You see, Monroe Tucker (His friends nicknamed him Tommy and this does make a difference later on.) or Tommy, Sr., served his country in World War II. When he came back to the states, he started working for the railroad, but that just didn't pan out. "My nerves went haywire, doctors says do something else and I got into this business," he says. This business is Tucker's Barbeque. With a mess sergeant's background behind him, Tommy, Sr., opened up shop in 1947 and he's served his customers ever since.

He's even brought his son Tommy, Jr. (and that is his real name), into the business. And I gotta say what tickles me most when I walk into Tucker's restaurant is these two guys decked out in dress shirts (The day I went, one wore pink and the other wore green,), ties, and when it's chilly, sweaters. It's a father-son thing that started when the older Tommy got a lesson in business decades ago. "An old man came up the counter and says, 'You've got a good clean business here. Why don't you dress the part?' Well, I got to thinking and I've been doing it ever since," explains Senior. It all makes sense because much like the era when men wore ties even to serve you lunch, it mimics the time when Big Red sat on the counter right along with the Goody's powder, when the owner greeted you with a big ole "Come on in here, buddy." And when you could still order up a Schlitz or make fun of a plastic gaudy pink pig starring at you with indignation. It's all still here…the plastic table clothes, the wood-paneled walls, and, oh yeah, plate after plate of great finger-lickin' barbeque.

Junior thinks the secret to the barbeque's success is its old-fashioned ingredients. "We make a sweet sauce, but we don't use cheap-grade ketchup. If you want to make a cheap sauce you can make it, but we don't." Senior adds, "We cook it about an hour and bring it to a boil"

What's barbeque without slaw? The Tuckers' recipe follows the same principles as their barbeque. "It's a good sweet slaw. We don't just throw in chopped cabbage; we use mayo and spices," says Tommy, Jr. And that's when Tommy, Sr., got worried: "Don't tell them about the spices," he says. "People call up and ask us all the time. I tell the women that call, 'Even if I told you, you wouldn't make it right.'"

Well, I'm not getting in the middle of that one, but what I will tell you is the barbeque is fine. But I must admit that I am not a pulled-pork connoisseur. What I dive into is the hamburger plate. We're talking a quarter-pound patty sitting on cheese, lettuce, tomatoes, and a heap of that slaw. Yup, slaw on the burger. It's so juicy and messy that it took me four napkins just to look presentable again. And a load of french fries comes on the side and not those frozen ones that come in boxes, but the genuine veggies that come out of Idaho dirt. "Before I ever went out on a date, I had to peel 100 pounds of potatoes," explains Junior. Well, nowadays there's no more peeling thanks to the flood of 1994. "During the flood we had no water, so we just left the skins on and people liked them," Tommy says.

All kinds of people have liked this stuff for generations; it's the kind of place where doctors sit at the counter with truck drivers, where Honda Accords and mud-boggin' trucks hang out in the parking lot.

David and Kim Stancile come for lunch three to five times a week. Now this food is good, but come on, it's not ranking in too high on the health food scale. The Stanciles do make sacrifices to balance the scales, so to speak. "Well, at night we eat steamed veggies at home. At lunch, we outdo ourselves," says Kim. The couple gets a real kick out of the drive-up—not the drive-thru but the drive-up. You can still pull in and Cedric will bring your meal on a tray to your window. "It's like a little taste of country homemade," says David.

And Tommy, Sr., has already been warned about tinkering with his success: "I have them come up to me and say, 'Tucker, don't change this business.'" With future Tuckers poised to take over this pork place, hopefully it never will.

Address: 4591 Broadway Street, Macon, Georgia

Directions: Tucker's sits practically at the end of Broadway Street in Macon, about 8 miles south of downtown Macon's Cherry Street. But it's also a stone's throw from Highway 247.

Hours: Tommy and Tommy sling barbeque every day except Sunday. They're open from 10:00 A.M. to 10:00 P.M., but they do keep the place open a bit later till 11:00 P.M. on Fridays and Saturdays.

Phone: (478) 788-9940

Prices: Back in 1947 a barbeque plate would of run you 25 cents, now its $4.95. My favorite, the Deluxe Burger, costs $3.65.

Extras: This is one of the only places in town where you can order Coke or Pepsi with your meal.

Since the writing of this book, Tommy, Sr., passed away at the age of eighty-six. He worked at Tucker's for sixty years of his life.

Doesn't this look good?

Chef Audrey in the kitchen.

Chef Audrey's Bistro and Bakery

The first time I met Chef Audrey I liked her. You can't help it; the stout Birmingham-born chef has a personality bigger than a billowy, ten-layer cake. It's part of the reason taking a trip to Chef Audrey's Bistro and Bakery is so much fun.

You can be pretty sure the chef's going to dazzle you with the food, but we'll get to that later. What you don't know is if Audrey's going to come out of the kitchen and burst into song— or show up at your table chuckling and playing with the kids. Robbie Martin knows about all of this firsthand; she works next door. "She's hilarious! We hear her cutting up. She's just livened up this shopping center."

Audrey takes it all in stride. "That's my thing. I try to meet everybody, go out and talk. I'm single. What else am I going to do?" she says with a smile.

Don't let her fool you: she's got a plateful of responsibilities. Bustling around in a tiny kitchen you can see from the dining room, Audrey puts her personal touches on every meal. "I make everything." She's a stickler for detail, which could be the reason every glass of water comes with a fresh sprig of mint, (She expects this in other restaurants too; I've seen her order it!) sodas stand in little homey 8-ounce bottles, and fresh flowers grace every white tablecloth.

Now lets talk about the food. The menu is chock full of novelties, things like wild mushroom tarts, spicy crab pitas, and roasted pork loin with curried peach sauce. Yeah, makes your mouth water. I had the best pastrami sandwich in my life when I stopped by. The meat was good, but Audrey slathered on a cayenne mayonnaise that made the meal. She does that with a lot of the stuff but blames her kids for the tinkering with spices and sauces. "My two sons were wild rambunctious boys." The kids had to endure yearly road trips from Birmingham to Baltimore, so Mom found some culinary entertainment. "Boys want to tear something apart or eat! So we would stop at Jewish or Italian delis and pick up different meats and cheeses. The game was for them to make the weirdest sandwich, but we still had to be able to eat it," she explains. The boys would throw on the jalapenos to try to heat things up, but when that didn't work they switched to cayenne. Audrey says they liked garlic so everyone's breath would stink! But remember the rule stood: you had to be able to eat it, and not every creation passed the test. "De is the weird one: he came up with a hotdog with sauerkraut, ketchup, mustard, and mayo on top. I told him we didn't vote for that one, baby!"

The boys may lay some claim to fame for the sandwiches, but the sweets are pure Audrey. When I asked for a dessert menu, she looked at me surprised and said, "I am the menu!" That's because things change daily. You might find a caramel cheesecake with chocolate gnash, a key lime pie piled high with whipped cream, or a white chocolate raspberry tart staring back at you from the case. Once again Robbie has the neighborly insight. "I have come in at closing and watched her make desserts. Everything's from scratch. I wish I could cook like that."

Well, for Audrey it's not just cooking. Her skills run a little deeper. "I'm here in the middle of the night and that's a spiritual thing… I start singing. It's all very therapeutic," she explains and then gave me an example. Get a mental picture of Audrey singing. "Oh, Lord, it's hard to be humble when you make desserts perfect each day!"

Humility is not her strong point, but for someone overflowing with tasty talent and a side of hearty smiles, some things are easy to overlook!

Address: 115 Margie Drive, Warner Robins, Georgia

Directions: From Macon, take 1-75 South to exit 146 and turn left. As you enter town, look for Margie Drive and hang a left. Right across from the Galleria Mall, you'll see the Jasmine Place Shopping Center.

Hours: Monday–Wednesday, 6:30 A.M.–11:00 A.M. (breakfast), 11:00 A.M.– 3:00 P.M. (lunch); Thursday–Saturday, 6:30 A.M.–11:00 A.M. (breakfast), 11:00 A.M.– 3:00 P.M. (lunch); 5:30 P.M.– 9:00 P.M. (dinner). Friday nights have live music!

Phone: (478) 953-7480

Website: www.chefaudrey.com

Prices: Lunch will run you around $7.00 for a sandwich and sides. Dinner lists between $14.00 and $17.00 for entrees.

Extras: Once a year on April 7 Chef Audrey opens up early to celebrate the restaurant's anniversary with a peanut butter breakfast. And remember this is the kind of place where you have to turn off your cell phone and pager when you walk in the door.

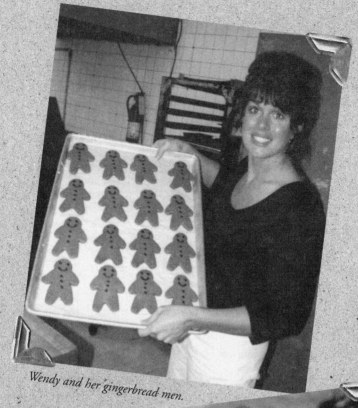

Wendy and her gingerbread men.

A lion cookie ready to go.

Wilson's Bakery

Wendy Wilson leads a pretty sweet life. When you own and run a bakery it's all part of the game.

Wilson's is deeply rooted in Warner Robins. The little shop opened up in the 1940s, but back then it had a different name, Nygaard's Pastry Shop. "He was a Norwegian baker. His family stayed in Norway and they had a bread bakery," Wendy explains.

Well, Wendy's own family had a floury past. Her grandpa made Meritta Bread deliveries and her dad baked up his own sugary future. "Dad had bakeries all over Central Georgia," she brags. "In fact, he was the first one to put a showcase in a grocery store bakery. I look at him doing things before they got popular." Wendy's dad liked the idea of folks getting doughnuts, cookies, and breads at the same place they did their grocery shopping. It seems crazy now, but back then folks didn't have super stores, so bakeries were pretty popular. Eventually the patriarch of the family needed more space to fill up his cases in Marshallville, Montezuma, and Fort Valley. He needed a kitchen, so he approached the most popular baker in town about making a deal. In 1979, the Nygaards sign came down and the Wilsons' sign went up. "I was thirteen when all of this transpired," Wendy says. "My dad was a big distribution dreamer. In due time, he realized this bakery was a handful." But he kept on and eventually let the grocery stores go and just concentrated on the store. Little did he know that the little girl who sat beside him as he visited all those display cases across Georgia had dreams of taking over the family business. In 1989, at the ripe old age of twenty, Wendy set out to put her stamp on the sugar. "Dad taught me the business and a work ethic. Mr. Nygaard taught me about good product," she beams.

Wendy carries a deep affection for the original baker in the building; she's still selling an original Isak Nygaard creation: finger nut cookies. Folks buy the little cookies by the dozen, and during the holidays Wendy says it's not unusual to sell 10,000 a week of the slim little treats with a pecan flavor. "Those are like what a Big Mac is to McDonalds," she says.

They are good, but so is everything that I tasted. I think my favorite cookie is the flower cookie. I've never tasted a softer cookie and one that just melts in your mouth. The oatmeal cookies are so moist they just ease apart sitting in your hands. And if you're the kind of person who likes to take a treat home for Rover, no problem. Wendy gets her 100-pound golden retriever to taste test the doggie treats she has for sale.

Amy McMillan says she hits this spot at least twice a week. "I'm not a sweet eater, but I like this. The cake is just so soft and moist," she exclaimed.

Amy likes the cakes, but one day she found herself at quite a crossroads over a certain delicacy. "A lady was just in here and she says she always stops for a doughnut and I bought the last one, so I gave her mine." Quite a generous act, especially when you come to find out all the doughnuts are made and, yes, fried daily and by hand. Wendy doesn't have any machinery cranking out the goods.

But she does have that spark of entrepreneurial spirit that came from her dad. You see, a good many of the folks that work at Wilson's are Hispanic. Wendy noticed every weekend that they would take road trips to Atlanta for their baked goods. It seemed strange since they worked with the very products they left town to find, so Wendy asked them what was up. They told her there is a whole menu of Hispanic baked goods that American bakeries and grocery stores just don't carry. Well, the flour popped in Wendy's head and she started carrying Mexican treats in the shop. They also have hot tamales, bollilo, and tres leches, which is a three-milk cake.

Wendy's feeling pretty good these days about keeping the tradition that started more than sixty years ago alive. She's sentimental and knows that for some folks walking through the door to Wilson's and down the road Panaderia the real treat is reconnecting with the past. "I think the most rewarding is when people come in and say, 'My dad brought me here when I was a young girl' or when people who have moved off and they come back to visit and say, 'Oh, you're still here.'"

Wilson's is still there; run by a woman who thinks the icing on the cake is carrying on the traditions of three generations of bakers.

Wilson's Bakery

Address: 1719 Watson Boulevard, Warner Robins, Georgia

Directions: From Macon, take I-75 South to exit 146 (Warner Robins/Centerville exit). Hang a left. You'll be on Watson Boulevard, so go approximately 8 miles down the road. Wilson's is located in the Miller Hills shopping center.

Hours: Monday–Friday, 6:00 A.M.–5:30 P.M., Saturday, 6:00 A.M.–3:00 P.M.

Phone: (478) 922-9300

Extras: They also have one of those cool photo cake machines that can reproduce any picture in a cake's icing!

Samples for you to snack on.

Priester's Pecans

Georgia is one of the top producers in the country when it comes to pecans. And folks at one restaurant have gone a little nutty over the snack themselves.

But this story actually began in Fort Deposit, Alabama. Back in the 1930s, Lee C. Priester owned and ran a gas station. Seventy years ago gas stations didn't carry giant drinks for $.89, lottery tickets, or sandwiches sitting in coolers. Nope, they had gas. But at Mr. Priester's station you could get some bagged pecans. Well, folks liked these Southern treats and the business took off. Today the family has two successful stores: one in Alabama and ours in Georgia, which began in 2002.

As you cruise down I-75, Priester's Pecans is hard to miss with its mammoth log cabin-like building. As a matter of fact a good many of this adventure's features are larger than life. A row of rocking chairs line the front porch and a 6-feet-high terra cotta man guards the front door and the sample table. "There are those that come in just to hit the sample bar, one gentleman will come in here and wipe out the honey glazed bowl three or four times a week," says Mary Skinner, a Priester's employee. She's seen it all, too, and as for the guy who dives into the freebies, well, she says when that happens most folks have the common courtesy of buying a few bags of goodies.

But the hard part for the customers comes in deciding which pecans to pick. You'll find pecan clusters, peach pecans, pecan divinity, pecan brittle, pecan fudge, pecan logs (didn't *Forrest Gump* have a line like this?)… Anyway, you get the idea. Then you've got all the other gooey goodies tempting your taste buds, things like white chocolate clusters, all kinds of pies, and chocolate bark. Even with all these choices, Mary says their best sellers have the least amount of ingredients. "People like the roasted and salted and the honey-glazed," she says, "but my favorite is the key lime. I'm the oddball."

She's not the only oddball. I loved the brushed and powdered bright-green nuts that remind you of Florida. And while a good many folks pile in for the pecans Mary says folks also stop in a few times a week for the country cooking.

Take for instance Bob Molton. When I met him, he was pushing aside the remnants of his fried chicken lunch and enjoying a bit of television on the big screen in one of the dining rooms. "I come three times a week because it's just good food," he says. Although he did give an insiders tip. "Friday's the best because they serve catfish!"

You do have to plan for these types of events. You see, meals at Priester's work like they may have at your house. Like at my house when I was growing up, Friday was always spaghetti night, Sunday some sort of roast, and so on. At Priester's, where you sit at heavy wooden painted dining room tables, operates much in the same manner. On Monday, you may get pork chops, but fried chicken is served hot every day. The meal also comes with a salad bar and a dessert bar, but we'll talk about dessert in just a few minutes.

The salad bar is fresh and basic except for a few extras like chicken salad, black olives, and some fantastic broccoli floret salad.

I'm not a huge meat eater, but the macaroni and cheese was gooey, cheesy, and ranked right up there with Mom's. They also had a very cheesy squash casserole with chunks of celery and carrots.

But enough of all that stuff that doesn't really matter if you've got a sweet tooth. As you might expect the dessert bar is full of stuff that didn't fall too far off the tree. Make sure you grab a slice of the chocolate pecan pie. It's great, and the plain chocolate pie was really rich and sinfully good, too. They've also got cakes and ice cream for you to indulge in. And a word to the wise: you'd better hit that pecan sample table before you sit down to eat because after you load up on all this country fare you're not going to feel like finishing off any bowls of treats.

Although Mary says they have great cooks, the lead cook didn't really come by this whole thing naturally. "The kitchen manager is from Alaska," she explains. "When one of the other women would add in some grease she would say, 'Hey, what are you doing?'"

Well, just like buttery popcorn isn't the best for you at the movie theatre, you probably don't go into a place like this thinking you're going to drop a few pounds, but if you want set a precedent for a positively tasty trip, stop by Priester's for a pecan or two or maybe a bowlful or nutty goodness.

Directions: Priester's Pecans is 1 mile from the Perry Ag Center at exit 134 off I-75. Coming from Macon, go south on I-75 and take a right off the exit. Priester's will be on the right.

Hours: The store is open seven days a week, 8:00 A.M.–6:00 P.M. The restaurant is open for lunch Monday through Saturday, 11:00 A.M.–2:00 P.M.; Sunday, 11:00 A.M.–3:00 P.M. Priester's caters as well.

Phone: (478) 987-6080

Website: www.priesters.com

Extras: Even though their main store is in Alabama, most of Priester's pecans come from Georgia growers.

Strangely enough, if you look at a map, you can draw a straight line between Priester's two stores: one in Perry and the other in Fort Deposit, Alabama, 35 miles south of Montgomery.

Georgia Bob.

The grill pit sits right outside the convenience store.

Georgia Bob's

When you have folks come to town, you might get a couple of grins when you pack them up and say, "We're going to the best barbeque place in town and it's inside a convenience store!"

Georgia Bob's sits alongside the Flash Foods on Russell Parkway in Warner Robins. His huge grill takes up part of the parking lot. Bob knows it's an unusual setting. "I knew I had to start somewhere and grow, and this is the busiest corner in Warner Robins," Bob explains.

This is a guy who knows two things for sure in life: where to put a business and how to barbeque. The latter runs in his blood. "My Grandfather barbequed for 8000 people every year back in the twenties." That's when Peach County held the annual Peach Blossom festival every year. Peaches took center stage and Bob's kin took over the attention when folks wanted a hearty meal. "He barbequed 200 hogs. He taught my uncle how to barbeque and my uncle taught me…"

Eight thousand people is a lot, but Bob has surpassed his gramps with a little restaurant that brings in tons of people every week. As a matter of fact, when I asked Bob about the total amount of meat he's grilling each week, the gentle guy with the easy smile had to pull out a calculator. "Well, we put out 2600 pounds of pork a week and 1000 pounds of ribs."

When you sit down at a booth with the bright sunshine flowing all over the red, white, and blue atmosphere it's easy to see why people make the trip. I gotta say barbeque is not my favorite fare, so whenever I'm in Warner Robins I make sure I take home a quart of Bob's chicken salad. It's meaty and just slightly sweet, a perfect between two pieces of bread with a pickle!

But a lot of folks stop by for the meat. Once you bite into the thick, juicy ribs, you get the idea someone threw a slab on the grill just for you during a Fourth of July picnic. They're smoky and succulent! And Bob says his Brunswick stew is different from any another stew recipe in Georgia: "Mine's made out of beef. Now some may say that's not stew, but it is." Truthfully, I don't know the difference between Georgia stew and stew from Tahiti, but I do know that a cup of this stuff is thick, hot, and has chunks of corn and meat staring right back up at you.

Now, if you like sauce, well, there's plenty to slather onto your plate. Bottles sit lined up and ready to go on the table. They're vinegar-based and come in mild, medium, and hot. I didn't bother with the puny stuff and went right for the hot. It had good flavor and only slightly warmed my taste buds with the heat.

If you can't make the trip to Georgia Bob's as soon as you read this book, don't worry, this guy doesn't plan to change. "We're not going to turn into a catfish house or a buffet, we barbeque," Bob says.

And with barbeque this good, it doesn't matter if you walk into a free-standing restaurant or a convenience store! One last thing: be sure to check out the banana pudding and the chocolate delight. Don't be scared of this chocolate concoction. It looks like a mess but it's delicious.

Address: 1882 Russel Parkway, Warner Robins, Georgia

Directions: From Macon, take I-75 South to exit 144 and turn east. You'll drive almost 5 miles to the corner of Houston Lake and Russell Parkway in Warner Robins. Georgia Bob's is right by the Flash Foods.

Phone: (478) 971-1341

Extras: Check out another restaurant, Danielle's, an upscale New Orleans bistro (971-4408) also owned by the Georgia Bob's family.

Georgia Bob's also does catering and you can buy their barbeque, desserts, and chicken salad in bulk quantities. In fact Bob says the Brunswick stew makes a nice dip for a weekend football game!

Georgia Bob's Famous Low-Carb Barbeque Sauce

1 13.3 ounces of Hellmann's Low-carb Ketchup

4 ounces vinegar

12 packs of Splenda sweetener

1 teaspoon black pepper

2 ounces mustard

Place in bowl or bottle and shake thoroughly. Use a squeeze bottle for storage and dispensing.

Plate of barbeque.

Priscilla, Ann, and Ernest.

Cakes packaged and ready to go.

Ann's Deli

At Ann's Deli, you get a lot more than lunch. You can sit down to a good meal sandwiched in with a history lesson and a side order of conversation with the locals.

The shop occupies a space where the folks in Forsyth have walked in ringing the little bell over the door for years. The big, yellow-brick building housed the town's soda shop and drug store.

Today you can't get a prescription filled, but it still has the same feeling of decades past with tons of black-and-white pictures hanging on the walls, and the soda fountain still secure on the back wall.

Speaking of ice cream, Ann's does specialize in desserts. Sure, she'll scoop up a creamy sundae for you, but if you're in the mood for something different go for something baked. The woman does almost forty different kinds of cakes and pies. They line the counter, tempting you right off the bat. You'll find everything from Coca Cola cake to cherry cheese pie, and a lemon tart cake jockeys for your attention right alongside the chocolate chocolate cake.

Ann knows cake and any number of other goodies from her years in the kitchen. This shy woman lost her mom when Ann turned twenty-seven. It's sad, but she kept the warm memories of time the two shared: "Mom always baked. I baked on Christmas, and I told my husband I was going to open up a place that had desserts."

And so she did. The CVS chain bought the old original drug store, but when they moved out the space came open for Ann. It's bright and airy decked out in happy colors with a huge pegboard still lining one side of the building.

Just a few feet away from that backdrop, I found Priscilla Grant Doster and Ernest Jackson sitting at their usual table at Ann's. The couple eats here a few times a week. They say all they have to do is look around to feel like they're sitting at home. "The pictures in the back are military and all the people that grew up here or are still here," Priscilla explains. "The sailor next to the flag on the left side in the middle, that's Ernest. He had lots of hair back then." Ernest still has some hair and the good looks of his younger days.

We all sat around and talked over lunch. Ernest and Priscilla's lasagna came slathered in gooey cheese. I had the club sandwich. Ann says it's one of their specialties and it's no wonder. This triple decker sat on the plate with crispy bacon and just the right amount of mayonnaise. Ann says there is another secret: "We use good meats, just Boars Head," she says with pride.

Dessert sparked a lot of debate on the choices. Once again I opted for the favorite on the menu: the girdle buster. And I've gotta say, after having the soft, fluffy, gooey pudding-like bowlful of chocolate with whipped cream and cherry I don't think I can order anything else. Ann says it's also made with cream cheese, which may explain why it's so addictive. We also ordered the pineapple cream cheese cake. Now pineapple isn't my thing, but Priscilla loves this incredibly moist and fruity dessert.

If you want to stop by Ann's, make sure you check what day of the week you make your visit. Some days are livelier than others. "You should come by on a Monday or a Friday. Everybody's just talking back and forth," Ernest explains. "People that aren't from here sit at the outside tables because everyone has certain tables."

Don't be alarmed. These are nice folks who just do things the same way each day. Visitors are more than welcome to join in the conversations and you never know if you may give a shout out to the mayor or maybe a local football coach. It really is like having a meal with your neighbors—inside a time capsule. Ann's may offer folks different things inside its walls but always with the same hometown charm that you can only get in a small town.

Directions: From Macon, head north towards Atlanta on I-75. Forsyth is less than a half an hour up the interstate. Take exit 187, turn left and follow that road all the way into town square. Ann's Deli is located at 33 West Johnson Street right across from city hall.

Phone: (478) 994-4493

Inside view of the restaurant.

Maxine stirring the pots.

A lunch plate.

The Bear's Den

Now if you checked out the chapter on Bond Swamp yet (page 171), you'll know wildlife lives pretty darn close to the big city of Macon. Ironically, a few years back a black bear did make his way into town. "My auntie saw the bear," recalls Maxine Roberson , who's been cooking wonderful food for fifteen years. The furry guy might have been trying to make his way to a place serving some of the best home cooking in town and bearing his namesake: The Bear's Den!

The Bear's Den is well known in these parts for their moist, crispy fried chicken (which you can start to smell as soon as you hit the sidewalk outside), their heavenly desserts, and Maxine's gummy gooey macaroni and cheese.

Betty Marshall started the place back in 1989. She converted a tiny yellow grocery store with a red roof into a restaurant. "It was a dump, I wish you could of seen it," she says. Well, Betty would know. She ran her own grocery store up the road on Hill Street, but she saw a need in the neighborhood for something more. "Well, there was nowhere to eat around here. I just wanted something different," she says. "I love to cook—I always have—and I was tired of the grocery business. It was seven days a week. This is only five."

Betty had to name her place. She wanted to call the quaint culinary kitchen the Corner Café, but then her husband had an idea. "He says, 'You ought to name it the Bear's Den because of you've got the Mercer Bears and the Lanier Bears [in Macon].'" The high school that housed the Lanier Bears eventually turned into the Central Chargers, but the fighting Mercer Bears on the nearby university campus do still bring in a lot of business for Betty.

As a matter of fact, I stopped in on a Tuesday and it took time to find a seat in the cozy dining room that has sunshine streaming in and forest-green walls. And each day, a diverse crowd sits down at noon to enjoy the food.

It's a meat and two veggies kind of place, I had the chicken, very tasty macaroni and cheese that made me consider just ordering a vat of the stuff next time, and corn fritters that were so sweet and light I almost counted them as a second dessert.

And speaking of desserts, those are what Betty specializes in. You can't walk in without opting for a slice of red velvet cake, key lime cake, or pecan pie. I chose the turtle cheesecake. It tasted like custard and it came with a generous serving of rich chocolate on top lined with whipped cream. Oh yeah, and it sat on a thin layer of caramel. It makes my mouth water just writing about it!!

Betty puts out a bountiful array of sweets every day, but Monday through Friday is a set schedule for the main meal. For example, Tuesday is chicken parmesan and baked chicken. Thursday is hamburger steak and lasagna, but fried chicken headlines the menu every day of the week. Betty says she tries not to tinker with the menu too much because folks get upset. "As soon as you take something off someone will complain and say, 'That was my favorite,'" she explains.

Maxine's made her creations a favorite for sixteen years and she's Betty's right-hand cook. When you walk in, you can see her stirring up the big pots that smell like a family kitchen on Thanksgiving afternoon. "She's like all cooks; she's going to put her touch to it," Betty says. "She doesn't measure anything; she just puts it together."

Maxine says back in 1990 when she first began she followed the recipes, but then she got a little creative. "Well, with the macaroni and cheese I just started adding more ingredients to it. More butter, more milk, and more cheese," she says. Now I figured you can never have too much cheese, but Maxine says you can. It's all about the right blends in the pan. "We changed the broccoli casserole, too; we cut down on the butter and onions and added cream of chicken soup."

Her changes worked, and with Betty, Maxine, and the rest of the crew serving up such fine food every day, you might consider hibernating at their little restaurant all year long.

Directions: From I-75 North, take a left off exit 167 onto Riverside Drive. At the second light, take a right onto College Street. After a number of lights, make a left on Oglethorpe Street. The Bear's Den is on your left at 1191 Oglethorpe Street.

Phone: (478) 745-9909

Hours: Monday–Friday, 10:30 A.M.–3:00 P.M.

Extras: A meat and two veggies with a bread will run you $5.95. You can get a veggie plate for a couple bucks less and desserts ring in at a buck and a half. Betty also does catering and sells whole cakes and pies. Also, there's a take-out shop if you don't want to eat in the restaurant.

The Bear's Den.

Jack's.

Debbie McClendon with a couple of burgers.

Minute Grill and Jack's Hamburgers

The folks who live in Dublin can tell you a tale of two hamburger stands. These two local diners serve up a bounty of bite-sized burgers within a block of each other and both stands have been around for years.

Let's start with the Minute Grill. It's more of a walk-in restaurant with a décor that celebrates the sixties. Elvis posters share wall space with old Braves pennants, and yearbooks from decades ago sit next to the ketchup dispenser for folks who want to relive the good ole days.

There's a reason Donna Shinholster Kennedy has a special place in her heart for the sixties. "My parents bought the restaurant August 5, 1963," explains Donna. There are not too many days that go by that you won't find the younger entrepreneur behind the counter serving the famous food just like her parents did.

Right now, folks will wait in a line that snakes out the door for the bold little burgers, but the menu has changed through the years. The previous owners served full-course dinners. "Well, we had a fire in 1967 and my parents reduced the menu," Donna reminisced. "They kept the homemade chili and the homemade fries."

They kept the good stuff. The french fries come piping hot and with a crunchy batter. The chili comes by the bowl or as an extra touch on a scramble burger or a scramble dog. The hamburgers get dunked in a special sauce and sandwiched between velvety-soft steamed buns.

I sat at the counter with Betsy Thomas who ducked in for the special indulgence. "I compare these to Krystal's, but they're much better," she says. "When I think about Dublin, I think about the Minute Grill. I don't know anywhere else you can get fries like this," she added.

The fries are special, but walk ten steps out the door to the Minute Grill and you'll run into Jack's Hamburgers. This is more of an open-air stand where the grill runs the length of the place and patrons sit at a countertop to watch the burgers sizzle. The hamburgers may look like the ones at the Minute Grill, but hold on: these little guys come with a little more of a kick. Homemade hot sauce even sits at the bar, but Debbie McClendon is ready to douse the flames by pouring you a big cold glass of chocolate milk to go along with your order.

This restaurant has also stood the test of time. Debbie's been taking folks orders for twenty-six years at Jack's. "Older men and older ladies come in here a lot," she says. "Most times I can tell you what they eat but not their name."

Greg Newsome is a third generation customer at Jack's. "Dublin's changed a lot over the last few years but this is an original. It's the atmosphere of these places. It's like walking into your own home," he says. Greg can remember sliding up to the bar as a little boy for a burger. "These here with chocolate milk is real good," he says. "That's what my granddaddy used to have."

People feel passionately about these two places. But there seems to be plenty of room for both of these restaurants. And just like in the good old days, both owners foster a neighborly love towards each other. "If they need to borrow something, then we'll go over or they'll loan us whatever we need also," Donna says.

Deborah agrees. "We're still friends. We're competitors, but we're friends."

The Minute Grill

Directions: Traveling east on I-16, take a right off of exit 51 onto US Highway 441. The grill is located at the intersection of Highway 441 and US Highway 80 on the courthouse square.

Hours: Monday, Thursday, and Friday, 8:00 A.M.–5:00 P.M.; Tuesday and Wednesday, 8:00 A.M.–3:00 P.M.; Saturday, 10:00 A.M.–3:00 P.M. Closed on Sundays

Phone: (478) 272-9956

Jack's Hamburgers

Directions: Look across the street from the Minute Grill.

Phone: No phone here at Jack's.

Christian in the kitchen.

Giant scallops are a menu favorite.

The Back Burner

Over the last ten years or so, Macon has seen an influx of fine dining restaurants come to town. We're lucky because those of us who like to go out for a good meal didn't always have too many choices. That's where one man saw an opportunity. But let's start at the very beginning.

Christian Losito grew up 18 miles from the Italian border in Nice (pronounced "niece"), France. His parents owned a restaurant, so cooking is in his blood. "I would come home from school and sit and watch my Mom," he says. "I would take some flour and make a cake."

Those skills matured into a culinary career, and Christian found himself in Macon putting his touch on the City Club back in 1994. He worked three years downtown and then figured this might be the town to open up his own place. "I looked around and there weren't too many good restaurants in town except for Natalia's," he recalled. "My brother says, 'If you don't open something now, someone will beat you to it!'"

Christian and his wife looked around and they found a spot in Ingleside Village called the Sassafras Tea Room. "It was partly an antiques store and they served quiche for lunch. They didn't have any air conditioning and it was a dirt parking lot," he says. Christian cut a deal with the tea room's owners and now the little house is chock full of some of the best food in town.

We sat down with some friends one night and, as Celeste pointed out, "This is eating." When you walk in, you'll be impressed by the tablecloths and fresh flowers on every table (They don't have any booths.). The restaurant is quite literally a house with little nooks and crannies for intimate evenings with friends. Our friend Wayne says the Green Room is his favorite. Interesting art hangs in the candlelight, accentuated by bright and colorful walls and the napkins stand at attention folded in fans waiting to go into service.

For appetizers, we all sampled each other's plate, tasting carrot bisque, escargot, and mussels bathed in a white garlic sauce. Christian dresses up his tender crab cakes with shaved carrot. I wasn't going to waste any time on the bread, but when it hit the table I simply couldn't resist! It comes out fiery hot and soft and served in panini square wedges.

As for our main meal, this may be a fine dining experience but don't expect fru fru portions to come out of the kitchen. "I've seen a lot of restaurants where there are a lot of decorations on the plate. You don't want your customers to leave hungry," Christian reasoned.

The huge caramelized scallops and the veal tasted extraordinary, but the halibut turned out to be a table favorite. "The fish are our trademark," Christian explains. "The sea bass and halibut are simple to make but very good. They are sautéed and seared with a handful of crushed tomatoes, some capers, and olives. Then you add salt and pepper, some white wine, and let it simmer."

Christian is pretty true to what he calls his southern French cuisine roots. But since he also does all the cooking , he likes to mix things up on the menu. "We will do stuff nobody else does like rabbit venison and osso bucco (It's veal shank; I had to ask.)! The Frenchmen does command the kitchen, but when it comes to dessert he's hands off. That's Chantel Crespi's department. This short German woman weaves all kinds of wonderful concoctions together for you to finish off the night. Our party couldn't hold back, so we ordered the tiramasu, the crepes suzette, a napoleon, some chocolate mousse, and the raspberry sorbet. Now, we did have eight people at the table, so it made sampling easy. I don't know what you'd do if you actually have to choose one thing off the menu! The sorbet was so fresh it tasted like Chantel had just ground up the berries from a backyard garden. And my favorite, the napoleon, is about as large as a city block. As a matter of fact, they serve it with a steak knife so you won't have any problems cutting through the powdery layers. If you want more of a production, order the crepes: Chantel wheels out the cart and fires them up right by the table.

During your meal, expect to see Christian stopping by to see how you're doing. This guy loves running a restaurant, and he still loves cooking and creating. He even whips things up on his days off. "I believe if you don't like to eat it's hard to be a good cook."

Well, not only is he a good cook, but he's quite the gentleman, a gentleman inviting you into his home every night for quite a magical experience.

Directions: Going north on I-75, take exit 167, go straight across Riverside Drive down Pierce Avenue until you hit Ingleside Avenue. Take a left onto Ingleside and look to the right after the second light. It's located right behind Ocmulgee Arts at 2242 Ingleside Avenue.

Hours: Open for lunch and dinner Tuesday through Saturday. Christian takes Sundays and Mondays off from the kitchen. Dinner is served between 6:00 P.M. and 9:30 P.M. Although Christians says if you have to come earlier because of something pressing like a theatre engagement, that's okay! The restaurant closes for Fourth of July and Christmas. They also close down about ten days in January for vacation.

Phone: (478) 746-3336

Prices: Lunch will run you $13.00 for an entrée. This includes a salad and beverage. Dinners run in the price range of $20.00 to $25.00 for entrées and one of Chantel's wonderful desserts will run in the $6.00 to $7.00 dollar range.

Extras: Reservations are recommended. Christian says he hates to wait anywhere to eat a meal and he feels you shouldn't have to wait either.

Cox Capitol Theatre.

Cox Capitol Theatre

"It's just different. It's not your average movie experience."
Elli Gauthier isn't kidding. She runs the Cox Capitol Theatre. It's
a place where you can catch a flick, chomp down on some great
pizza, or jam out with the latest band to pass through town.

The Capitol originally opened up as a Macon bank back in
1897. It changed hands a few times and found its niche as a theatre that stood as a centerpiece in town in the 1920s. You can still
see an old black-and-white shot of the place in the lobby today.

In 1975, the Capitol closed its doors and the place sat
dormant and depressed for a few decades. "The floor rotted and
with the ceiling gone it had been raining in here for thirty years,"
Gauthier explains.

Investors took a shine to the property and brought the land-
mark back to life. It reopened in 2006 still showing off some of its
magic. "One cool thing is the stage lights. When the workers came
in to start the renovations, the lights just came on after thirty
years. The only thing they had to change were a couple of light
bulbs," Gauthier exclaims with wonder in her eyes.

But don't worry, those stage lights still shine down on a building that's kept its nineteenth-century charm. You'll see ornate
detail on the walls and a big golden C that crowns the top of the
screen. Spanish balconies also bookend the stage: "We keep the
go-go dancers in there," Gauthier jokes. She's kidding. This place
is totally kid friendly. They even run G-rated movies every week
for the tiny tot popcorn eaters.

But the beauty of this place is you don't have to just settle on
the typical theatre snacks. Second Street Pizza, which is the sister

restaurant to Ingleside Pizza, puts out a full menu for you to nibble on during the show.

"It's a little bit different than Ingleside," owner Tina Dickson says. "The crust is going to be crunchier and we make it thinner than at our Ingleside location." They also turn out jalapeno poppers, corn doggies, and thick loaded subs for you to sample while you're watching the movie. Just don't look for one thing on the menu. "We don't have chicken wings because I don't want to dig bones out of the chairs," Tina says emphatically.

The Capitol is laid out into three main areas. Upstairs they discourage you from eating, but you do get a stadium view of the screen and stage. Downstairs big cushiony executive-like chairs line bar like tables for you to enjoy your food. And when I say cushiony I mean cushiony. You just kind of melt into the fabric when you take a seat. "Yeah, those are the first to fill up. People like the pink seats," Gauthier says. Then just in front of those pink chairs is the area with full-service tables where waitresses come and take your order. In the dark, you may just think they're tables and chairs, but with the lights on you may find the décor strangely familiar. "All of this furniture came from a hotel that was closing down. Some of the tables that doubled as desks still have power inputs in the back, but people are comfy," Gauthier says.

The comfy furniture goes along with the warm memories folks have fostered for this movie house that came back to life. Gauthier says people constantly share their stories from the theater's past: "One guy said, 'You know, I took my first date here to see *Mary Poppins*. All the time I'm getting stories. One man emailed me from California the other day and said he used to be a ticket taker when it first opened up."

Back in the twenties the Capitol stood as a hub for local entertainment, but now it's time for the second act. So check out the show, and make sure you bring your appetite.

Cox Capitol Theatre

Address: 382 Second Street, Macon, Georgia.

Directions: From I-75, take exit 165 to get on I-16. From
there, you'll want the second exit, which is ironically the 2nd
Street exit. Take a right onto Riverside Drive and then another
right at the next red light onto 2nd Street. Drive two blocks and
you'll see the theatre on the left at the corner of 2nd Street and
Cherry.

Hours: Check out the website for show times. They usually
run movies that have just left mainstream theatres.

Phone: (478) 257-6391

Website: www.coxcapitoltheatre.com

Extras: Thursday night is concert night and Gauthier says they
bring in national acts like Drive By Truckers, Hank Williams III,
and the Dirty Dozen Brass Band. Look for the annual Film
Festival to happen in late February to early March.

2nd Street Pizza

Phone: (478) 257-6392

Hours: You don't have to watch a movie to grab some pizza at
2nd Street. They are open for lunch Monday through Friday,
11:00 A.M.–2:00 P.M. Dinner goes out the door Wednesday
through Sunday with the kitchen staying open a little later on the
weekends. Tina's crew takes off Monday and Tuesday nights.

Festivals and Fun

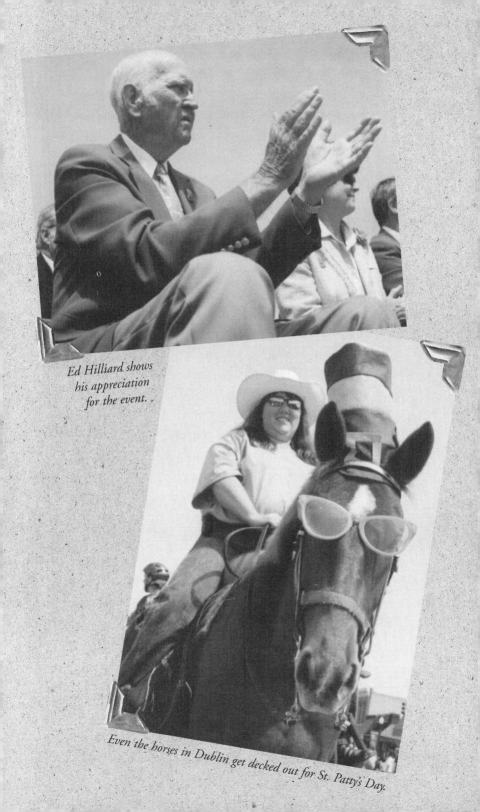

Ed Hilliard shows
his appreciation
for the event.

Even the horses in Dublin get decked out for St. Patty's Day.

Dublin St. Patrick's Day Festival

You don't have to make a beeline for Limerick to find the luck of the Irish. Every March, a town off I-16 celebrates their namesake in the Big Dublin St. Patrick's Day Festival.

Now believe it or not, you would think this kind of a celebration would come as a no-brainer to a town named Dublin. But it actually took a little ingenuity by some guys at the local radio station and the town's paper. Back in 1966, "[w]e had disc jockeys screamin' and yellin' because Dublin didn't do anything on St. Patrick's Day!" says Ed Hilliard. Hilliard and his friend Dick Killebrew who worked WMLT decided to get something started, so they got the *Courier Herald* on board and the festival came to be.

Killebrew has passed away, but Hilliard, at the age of seventy-eight, still decks out in his green blazer for plenty of appearances. But don't expect this quiet guy with a little twinkle in his eye to take much credit for the sea of green that blankets the town. "I don't like riding in those cars [at the parade]; all them people looking at you. Lord have mercy," he explains. Although he's a bit bashful, the World War II veteran without a bit of Irish in his past is proud and figures all this green is paying off in his life. "I'm seventy-eight. Must have a little luck somewhere!"

Hilliard doesn't have to organize things anymore; there's a sea of volunteers who stage almost fifty events each year. The men work through the Order of the Shillelagh and the women have their own group, the Order of the Blarney Stone.

The St. Pats chairman serves for one year and that's how I met Sue Carr. Now admittedly, she doesn't own a Blarney Stone, she can't spell shillelagh (But really, who could off the cuff?) and her only claim to Irish fame is her husband's side of the family, but despite all that if I met a leprechaun in person it would resemble Sue. She took me all around in a car decked out with green bows on the side mirrors and explained the charm of the festival: "We take pride in it being a small town. It's a fun place to raise your family. We moved to Atlanta for a while and moved back here to raise our child."

It makes sense. At the Dublin St. Patrick's Day festival, you're not going to find the drunken boisterousness that happen a few miles down the road in Savannah. No, this is more of the kind of place where kids run free looking for green popcorn and pancakes.

You really do have to do some planning ahead of time to hit all of the events you want to see. Some of the highlights include the Grand Ball, the irish corned beef and cabbage dinner, the leprechaun road race, the pancake dinner, and the Miss Emerald City Pageant. But thousands show up for Super Saturday. That's when the parade marches down the street. Among the bands, floats, and fun, I actually spotted a green horse! After that, folks meander on over to the big arts and crafts fair. Among the four-leafed clovers and green attire, you never know what you'll find.

Tammie Taylor bought a beautiful wooden bowl and told me an interesting story about a green encounter. "I had some lemonade and it was green," she says. "I'm like, 'What is this? I asked for lemonade.' But I thought it was very good and pretty creative," she says as she chuckled about the whole thing.

You can bank on green, but for us folks used to grits and iced tea you may find some unusual cuisine. Inside the park on Super Saturday, check out Cayden's Corner. The authentic crew serves up potatoes, pancakes, soda, bread, and scones. They even have some drinks that come from the green land: mint ice tea and Ribina, a drink that's a little tart and sweet. I asked James White about the green flapjacks. "We make them with potatoes, tarragagon, flour, pepper, and heavy cream," he explains. "It's an American-Irish dish more than anything else served with applesauce and sour cream." It couldn't be any more American than the green dill pickles. Folks who seem apprehensive about the spuds usually go for those.

And that's okay because in the land of leprechauns—in Dublin, Georgia—in the month of March, you gotta think God looks down with Irish eyes a smiling.

Dates: You'll find events stacked up on the calendar all throughout the month of March.

Directions: From Macon, take I-16 towards another American-Irish town, Savannah. Hang a left off exit 51 and follow it to Dublin.

Phone: Dublin-Laurens County Chamber of Commerce (478) 272-5546

Website: www.saintpatricksfestival.com

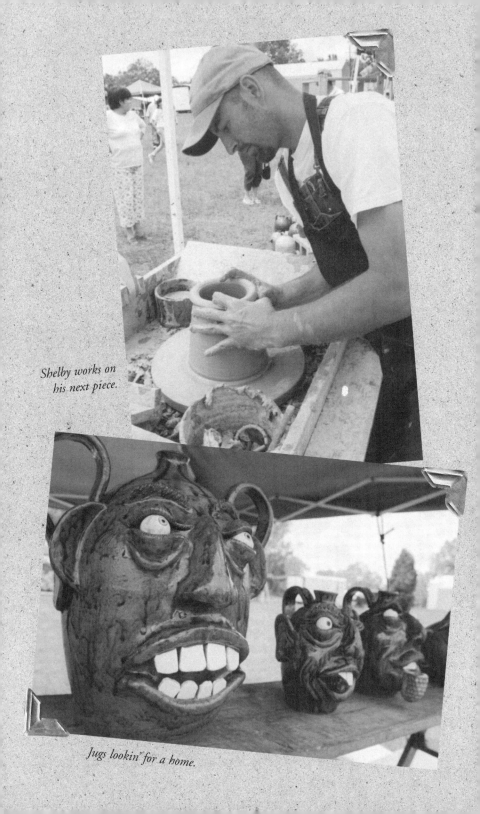

Shelby works on his next piece.

Jugs lookin' for a home.

The Brown Jug Festival

Before Tupperware, CorningWare, Gladware, and, yes, even Stoneware, folks had to have containers for their stuff.

That's where the heritage of Crawford County comes into play. Every spring on a wide green field behind the Crawford County Courthouse, the locals celebrate their history with the Georgia Brown Jug Festival.

The celebration is only a couple of years old, but the tradition dates back a ways in history. Mark Merritt, whose family has a reputation for churning out beautiful pieces throughout time, says back in the mid 1800s folks started discovering Crawford County just had the right kind of clay to make pottery. "Clay formed along the fall line, here the rocks stop and they turn sandy."

Now, artists took notice, but back then folks didn't have a whole lot of leisure time. Most things they did had a purpose and filled a need in life. So they molded the clay into butter churns, bean pots, water jugs, syrup jugs, and—hold your breath—even whiskey jugs. Think about it. No one had glass or plastic so the clay is what they used. They also didn't have a rainbow of colors to work with, so most of the pieces had dark brown, black, or gray glazes. That's what the authentic stuff looks like.

When you go to the festival, a lot of potters have their work for sale in an arts and crafts area. It's beautiful stuff. You'll also see typical festival fare. While you comb through the clay, you can munch on giant chocolate chip cookies, fish sandwiches, or home-made banana walnut bread. But look beyond that for the real history lesson. The most expensive and rare pieces sit inside a room in the new Crawford County Courthouse, where everyone whispers (Turns out really loud noises can make clay crack.).

That's where I met Pat Keller, a woman who explains the sentimental importance of the art form. "I believe there is a kind of immortality you can achieve for people if they can't achieve it for themselves," she says. Pat has a reverence for the families who sculpted giant jugs that have stood the test of time. She walked through the makeshift gallery showing off the pieces. The ones in full form are beautiful, but the folks in Crawford County really cherish the rare chipped off pieces that relate directly back to their land. Seems back then folks didn't really think that their butter churn would be worth something one day. "I bought a chunk of a face piece for a hundred dollars at a waste dump, I would never sell it now."

You can buy the artwork, but in this room be prepared to break out your checkbook. It works like an auction and some of the jugs go for some hefty Benjamins. "This is a Billy Merritt. It's cracked and chipped, but it will start at a thousand dollars," Pat explains. "It may or may not sell."

As with a lot of old-time techniques, you may think it's hard to sell the younger generation on the pottery. Well, twenty-six-year-old Shelby West is willing to carry the torch. I found him in the arts and crafts section pounding away on an authentic hand-made treadle wheel. For those who've never heard of a treadle wheel (myself included), it's an old-fashioned pottery wheel powered by your foot. Shelby says that while he could use a more modern contraption run on electricity, he has to consider necessity much as his ancestors did. "I like to collect pottery, but I couldn't afford it. So I figured if I could make stuff the way they did, everyone could afford it." So Shelby found some big ole pieces of oak, cut them, cleaned them, and, as he put it, just kind of figured it out. "It's cheaper and more authentic. Kind of heavy to move around though."

As a crowd gathered around Shelby's booth to watch the young man with the old soul work, he pondered his role: "I should have been born in 1850. I would've fit in better." He might have fit in but I think Shelby's right where he needs to be. After all now you have the chance to cherish the work of the past and watch the treasures of the future come to life right in front of your eyes.

Phone: For more information contact the Roberta/Crawford County Chamber of Commerce at (478) 836-3825 or (478) 836-3195.

Seasons: Each May.

Website: www.georgiajugfest.com

Extras: Part of the proceeds from the Georgia Brown Jug Festival go towards creating a pottery museum in Crawford County.

Shana stands next to the hearse buggy.

Downtown Barnesville during the festival.

Barnesville Buggy Days and More!

The little town of Barnesville has a lot of fun things going on that you can explore any time of the year, but the city really celebrates its heritage every third weekend in September. It's called Barnesville Buggy Days, which makes sense because in the late 1800s, before the Model T came along, this tiny town stood as one of the leading producers of the main form of transportation: the cart and buggy. "We were the largest buggy manufacturer center south of Cincinnati, Ohio," says Shana English, director of the Barnesville Old Jail Museum. Shana can talk history for hours, and even though she grew up in Michigan, she's the one you go to if you want to know anything about Barnesville's background. "Almost everyone was employed or had something to do with the buggies," she explains. "The cars came along and *pssswwhhhh*, by 1928 there wasn't a demand for parts anymore. The automobile took over." Afterwards, Barnesville began to rely on agriculture, but now every summer the town's inhabitants can count on tourism dollars as thousands walk the streets for the annual festival.

From birdhouses to belts, pottery to purses, mums to medieval helmets, the arts and crafts festival is typical fascinating fare. It runs along two streets through town and I must say my dog Salty did get a styling dog hat, and the humans in the group purchased a handmade wrought-iron hose holder and of course some kettle corn. It was also hard to hold back from the great funnel cakes and the plump sausage. Festivals usually have some sort of kid area, and I gotta tell you, I wanted to ditch the adult fun to hang out with the younger crowd. They had the chance to ride a bucking bronco, climb walls, and handle some go-cart racing!

And even though that's all a lot of fun, if history turns you on at all you've got to stop by the old jail, although keep in mind it's not really that ancient. "It started as a WPA project in 1938 and it was used up until 1992," Shana recounts. The jail takes up the second story of the building. Heavy iron bars with flaking yellow paint sit rooted to the floor. It's a plain depressing site complete with three isolation cells with slots in the steel where guards slid in the food. Graffiti on the walls livens the place up, and though some of it went up after the prisoners left, it adds ambience for the haunted house that happens here in October. And believe it or not some folks who used to call the jail home come by and reminisce. "They bring kids, sweethearts, and say, 'I was in this.' I just look at them kind of funny," Shana says.

Well, the past prisoners pale in number compared to the folks who stop in for a history lesson. You see, the sheriff used to live on the first floor, but now his living quarters provide a walk down Barnesville's memory lane. Shana has compiled quite a few interesting artifacts, all with ties to the city. "This glass hearse is our jewel," Shana explains with pride. It's amazing to look at this long pine buggy with a glass-enclosed belly that took coffins down the road to the cemetery. "The hearse was made in 1890 at a factory on Forsyth Street in Barnesville, and it would ride through town drawn by four white horses," Shana explains.

You'll also see a Barnesville fire truck that came from Buffalo, New York. Decades ago, drivers rode buggy style and Shana says the mayor and fire chief had quite a time riding through a blizzard to get back home to the warm South.

An actual safe from the largest buggy company, Jackson B. Smith, sits hunkered down in a corner. And there's quite a bit of history on Gordon College, which still operates in the area. Outside in an old gin house you can check out more old buggies and some farm equipment. It's the kind of stuff you don't see every day. "[Visitors] love it, but you wouldn't come in the door if you didn't like old."

Shana can spout stories and facts about everything in the museum, but she can even do one better than that if you're interested in your own history. In this Michigan State grad's office sits pounds and pounds of city and county records. She's got court and criminal documents, census figures, old newspapers, and even some slave and Confederate papers. Armed with all that info, Shana will research any family genealogy questions you may have. Of course, your kin needs to have some sort of tie to Central Georgia to put Shana to work on your family tree.

The Barnesville Buggy Days Festival may wheel you into this town of the present, but make sure you check out the past. The mistress of the jail has all kinds of historical surprises for you to explore.

Barnesville Buggy Days

Seasons: Third weekend of September
Phone: Barnesville Chamber of Commerce, (770) 358-5884
Website: www.barnesville.org

Barnesville Old Jail Museum and Archives

Directions: From Macon, take I-75 North to exit 201, turning left off the exit toward Barnesville. Go straight and ignore the truck bypass. You'll enter downtown Barnesville and go through a single traffic light. Two blocks on the left sits the Lamar County Courthouse. The museum and jail are located directly behind.

Hours: Wednesday, 10:00 A.M.–5:00 P.M.; Saturday, 10:00 A.M.–2:00 P.M.; Sunday, 2:00 P.M.–5:00 P.M.

Phone: (770) 358-0150
E-mail: ojmuseum@yahoo.com
Prices: There is a $1.00 fee to tour the jail and museum.

Bag of onions for sale from Stanley Farms.

Onions coming off the production line.

Vidalia Onion Festival

You won't find much culinary crying in Vidalia, Georgia. "I love the festival; everyone gets so happy." Elizabeth Harvill is with the Vidalia Onion Convention and Visitors Bureau. "On the wall of our office it says you only cry when they're gone."

Makes sense. About sixty years ago, a Toombs County farmer pulled out his crop and found out his onions didn't have the normal sting. They tasted much sweeter. Old Mose Coleman figured he had something so he started selling those Vidalia onions at a premium price. It caught on and other farmers joined in on the act. As a matter of fact, a historical marker still sits at the Krystal hamburger restaurant where the first onions came out of the ground. Now to carry the special title of Vidalia onion the little orbs have to be grown in this area, about a twenty-county region.

R. T. Stanley, Jr., and his family stamp their name on one brand of onions going out the doors in bright red bags. "We've got about 1000 acres and I've been in the business, oh, about twenty years," he says with a grin. "I quit counting after that." I quizzed him on why no one else on the planet can duplicate what comes out of this rural Georgia area. "Well, it's according to how you treat them, fertilize them, water 'em, and the sulfur content," he explains.

The sulfur mixes in with sandy soil and a huge dollop of Georgia sun beating down on the fields and the outcome is this special onion. I asked R.T. if these conditions only apply to the crop carrying the town's name. "Yes, peanuts come out a lot sweeter. Makes some good sweet peanut butter," he says.

The festival is a lot younger than the onion. The festivities began in 1977 when the Vidalia women's club thought the town needed to celebrate its crowning crop. The fourth weekend of April, thousands of folks pour into the little town for a big arts and crafts festival, an onion cook off competition (one year chocolate dipped onion petals took home the prize), and a slew of other events.

They even have some high-flying visitors every year that buzz on in for the air show. A few times in the festival's history, the elite squad of the Blue Angels have made an appearance. "The whole town comes out to the grounds and it's a big picnic with fireworks and everything," says Pollyann Martin who grew up in Vidalia and is heavily involved in the festivities. She quickly told me to fit in and not sound like an out-of-towner. You first have to pronounce the town's name correctly. "It's not *Vidalia*. You drop the L," she explains, "so it comes out *Vida-ia*."

The town also has a mascot but don't look to him for language lessons on the onion. Yumion doesn't talk and to be quite honest he does look a little out of the ordinary. "Basically, small children do get a little scared, and they tend to cry when they first see him," Pollyann admitted. "But he loosens them right up and dances with them. He can really move, especially at the street party!" Well, that's a sight to see in itself. Work on this mental image: Yumion sprouted twenty-five years ago; he's as tall as an adult with a giant onion head that takes up half his body. He's got huge sweet eyes and a mouth that runs from side to side, smiling all the time.

The smile is something most folks in this town wear. After all, they have some pretty big bragging rights. "We used to compete with Walla Walla, Washington, on who had the sweeter onions. Well, we won of course," Pollyann says confidently.

Harvill had another story. "I saw a sign in Paris, France, when I was studying abroad and it said, 'Vidalia Onions sold right here,'" she reminisced. "I said, 'Take my picture. I can't believe it.'"

It's not hard to believe at all. Vidalia, Georgia, has a world-wide reputation for taking something with a little sting and growing it into a sweet all-around experience!

Directions: Take I-16 down past Dublin and start looking for the Vidalia exit. You will take a right off the ramp and head to town. It's about an hour and a half from Macon. (There are driving directions also on the website.)

Seasons: The Vidalia Onion Festival always hits on the fourth full weekend in April.

Phone: Vidalia Area Convention and Visitors Bureau, (912) 538-8687

Website: www.vidaliaonionfestival.com

Favorite Recipe

Cut out center of onions. Put in a pad of butter. Take a knife and pierce the rest of the onion and then pour Kahluha over it. Wrap it in aluminum foil and bake it for an hour at 325 degrees.

"You can almost eat this recipe as a dessert."—Pollyanna Martin ("I just enjoy eating it raw!"—R. T. Stanley, Jr.)

Kathleen getting ready to put out more books.

Overhead shot of the sale.

Friends of the Library Old Book Sale

Every year when the daffodils start to poke their bright yellow heads out of the soil, bookworms make an annual pilgrimage to Central City Park in Macon for the Friends of the Library Old Book Sale. Now, lots of towns and communities have these kinds of events to help out the local library, but Macon's claim to fame is that it puts out one of the largest literary spreads in the Southeast! The volunteers who run this thing are pretty much a humble bunch who wouldn't brag on their own. An independent source crunched the numbers for them. "Well, this year we advertised on Bookfinder.com," explains nine-year veteran Kathleen Melikian. "They asked us how many books we have and we told them 150,000, which we believe is a low estimate, and they came back and told us we're one of the largest."

When you go, you'll know these guys deserve the ranking. It's all set in the cavernous Central City Park Long Building. Think of it as a book lover's paradise. It's like a giant pile of leaves—you just get to dive right in! You can even find books marked for a quarter. I picked up a Dell first edition *Poker according to Maverick* paperback. For more refined tastes, you can head to the rare books section. But make sure you bring your checkbook as opposed to pocket change. These treasured books can run up to a thousand dollars. But most of the books run anywhere from fifty cents to three bucks.

It all sounds like fun, and it is, but Melikian warns that you may want to approach the whole thing with a sound strategy. "You can pick out the novices walking through the door because they don't bring anything to carry," she says with a smile. The sale does stack cardboard boxes around the perimeter for folks who come unprepared, but just look around, the veterans can get quite creative. Plenty of Red Flyer wagons go rolling by. Some folks feel those suitcases on wheels do the trick, and I even saw one woman who put her recycle bin on wheels. You get the idea. You're going to need something big, mobile, and ready to roll. Melikian had some more tips. "I never understood why people don't hire someone to stand in line for them," she says. "Kids are great for this. Now I am cheap. My kids never got more than lunch and the pleasure of my company when we came years ago."

Knowing Kathleen, I'm sure they got a great lunch and a gazillion books to boot for their efforts. But speaking of the line, it is daunting, especially on the first day of the sale. You may find yourself back on the sidewalk where folks wait for the doors to open in the first place. Six cashiers with helpers work constantly to ring up the sales, but when every person's got a boatload of stuff, well, you can imagine it takes sometime. But the line does move and some folks tend to make the best out of the situation. One jolly guy in a University of Georgia t-shirt asked if he could lease a corner of Pat Dunaway and Lea Owens's wagon as he waited behind them in line. They said no problem. "We're just having a good time and it's a chance to talk," Pat said.

The folks that buy wagonloads of books tend to have the giving spirit during the year. Melikian says 95 percent of the stuff you see on the tables is donated. Five percent comes from books the library retires off the shelves. "People with collections give them to us," she says. "This year a man whose wife passed away gave us over $300 worth of cross stitch kits. The man started to cry when he gave them to us because he just wanted someone to use them and they were exquisite."

Book people hold pages dear to their heart, and these volunteers put that same emotional love into setting up this sale every year. After putting in backbreaking time loading boxes and bringing them down to the park and hours tediously pricing every book, they'll only take one day off before they start the whole process over again. Melikian says a group of ladies began this tradition in 1969 and back then they had the sale at the old Westgate Mall. "I think we made about $1100 that year," she says. Now, they make considerably more. So when you go to the sale and hear that gravelly shooshing of boxes as they're pushed across the concrete floor, just think of the old books you'll have at home and the new books that will appear on the shelves at the library. It all works out for a happy ending to the story.

Phone: Friends of the Library, (478) 744-0824

Hours/Seasons: The sale is always the Thursday, Friday, and Saturday after Presidents' Day in February. When it starts on Thursday, people line up very early to get in the door. Melikian says one man always comes the night before and puts down his box to reserve his space. But don't worry too much about it; even with hundreds waiting to get in, it usually takes less than twenty minutes to get in the building.

Extras: If you would like to donate books, you may be able to claim it as a tax break. The Friends will give you a receipt for your donations. They also have a great need for volunteers to price books during the year and help out at the sale.

The Friends say they re-stack the shelves every day. And they do, but what really happens is they pull them up off the floor and put them on the tables. So be sure you peek on the ground at all the boxes that aren't as easy to see and just haven't found their place in the sun yet.

SUZANNE LAWLER

Ann horses around.

Racer on the track.

Hawkinsville Harness Racing

When you drive through the Hawkinsville, you immediately get the idea the town has an unmistakable pride concerning their winter tenants. The Trotters Inn welcomes folks in and just down the road you can get a meal at the Horseshoe Restaurant. Have you figured it out yet? Yup, every year when the weather turns bitterly cold and snowy in the north Yankees and Canadians come down to train their high-powered horses at the Hawkinsville Harness Horse Training Facility.

If you're not familiar with Harness Racing, no problem. The drivers actually sit on a cart-like contraption called a sulky. The driver sits in the back in a basic chair that's tilted up a little bit. But they don't have seatbelts, so it is really a dynamic situation of balance and teamwork between man and animal to get the job done. One of the only times you'll see bona fide racing, though, is during the Hawkinsville Harness Racing Festival.

Other than that, the horses just train day in and day out. "These babies that are training here will be in stake races all over the country." Ann Lilley sat down with me in a small office full of schedules, horse photos, and supplies. They had made the annual pilgrimage for years from the Great White North, so when the city started looking for track managers in 2002, they figured, "Well, we'll give it a whirl."

It's become a family affair that's growing through word of mouth. Their granddaughter runs the restaurant and more horse friends have moved down to take advantage of the wonderful weather and Southern landscape. "We started with 120 horses and now we're up to 250," Ann says proudly. "We have a big breeding farm in Canada and we're out racing all summer promoting Hawkinsville, inviting people to come, and take a look at it," she says.

You may wonder how the small town of Hawkinsville earned the title of "Harness Horse Capitol." Well, it seems the town's founders had foresight. In 1894, the Fair Association held the first official harness races. It took off, and although the state of Georgia doesn't allow betting on horses, the warm weather and red clay make a great combination for the teams to spend a chunk of their time training. And a little bit of that well-known Southern hospitality just provides the icing on the cake. "Everybody waves at you," Ann says, "and everyone's willing to just do anything for you."

The only thing that's a bit disappointing to Ann besides the gnats is the fact that unless it's festival time she says folks don't usually come out to see the show that happens every morning, as the horses trot around the track at practice. "A lot of people in Hawkinsville don't know they're welcome," Ann says. In fact, anyone can come out, take pictures, and just soak in the atmosphere. It is quite majestic to see these huge animals kicking up the clay as they work every day trying to shave seconds off their time on the track.

And even though it's too warm for the horses to workout in the afternoons feel free to stop by the barns. You may get a chance to talk to the groomers who may call a back tack room home. Feel free to ask the blacksmith questions as he's working. The only thing you need to be respectful of is touching the horses themselves without consulting an owner or a trainer. "The Standard Breeds are different than other horses; they're more excitable," Ann says. But Ann added the horse guys are usually receptive and willing to talk to you and answer questions.

Ann say it's hard work to run the facility, but don't bet on them leaving any time soon. "The funny thing is when you see something starting to blossom you hate to miss the flower. This is like home," Ann says with a warm smile.

Seasons: The official Harness Racing Festival happens every year on the first full weekend in April. It starts on Friday afternoon and runs all weekend. Sunday is a meet and greet for the horsemen. You can go out and visit the stalls October through April. And don't forget the crews usually take Sunday off.

Phone: (478) 892-9463

Website: www.georgiaharnesshorsetrainingfacility.com (Yeah, it's a long one.). You can also get information at the Hawkinsville Chamber of Commerce at hawkinsville.georgia.gov.

Extras: There is no charge to check out all the track action in the morning. They even have some bleachers so you can watch the horses go around and I've got to say it's pretty magical to see these athletes work out. If you decide to visit the barns, though, remember not to touch the horses unless you first talk with the trainer or the owner. And if you really want to hang with the locals grab breakfast at the Track Diner. It's open seven days a week and that's where the guys and gals go to fuel up before the day begins.

Stores, Tours, and More

Starting point of the sale at the New Perry Hotel.

Peaches to Beaches Yard Sale

Evelyn Simmons loves a good yard sale. She scours each one looking for quaint kitchen knick-knacks that will add to her collection. "I collect glass dishes and antique spatulas," she says. "We collect not to sell. They become our own personal treasures."

Folks who have that kind of spirit eventually make their way to the "World's Largest Yard Sale." This thing is a monster marathon that every year stretches 450 miles through quite a few states. Evelyn and her husband hopped in their car for this adventure back in 2000. "One day we had to go 100 miles off the route just to get a hotel," she recalled. The logistics didn't frustrate the couple one bit, as a matter of fact Evelyn immediately thought about staging that kind of sale in Central Georgia. "I talked to people and [the yard sale] really changed their economy because people not only shopped the sale, but they came back to enjoy for vacations to enjoy the quaintness of the towns," she says.

But just like a buyer wheeling and dealing for a prize, Evelyn had to sell people on her dream of starting a giant yard sale in Central Georgia. She envisioned a weekend where you could drive down the road seeing house after house with tables full of treasures lined up. "It took 2001 through 2004 to sell nine different counties," she says. "I personally met with the mayors and county commissions. I sold the concept and how it would fit each county individually and all together along the Golden Isles Parkway. My husband says I would argue with a fencepost!"

Her tenacity paid off and now the Peaches to Beaches Yard Sale stretches 172 miles in Georgia. On the second weekend in

March you'll find professional vendors and everyday folks setting out their stuff hoping you'll stop by. The sale runs for three days, although Evelyn says they don't stop folks from starting a little early on Thursday. The official kickoff point is in downtown Perry right by the New Perry Hotel. When I stopped by, I ran into some folks already scooping up some goods. "So far, so good. I've got a pot," Darlene Back says as she showed off her find. "I think this could really take off. We're at least going to Hawkinsville."

Pat Aldredge and her buddies from Christ Lutheran Church dressed up in cowboy hats and big smiles to sell the stuff in their booth. Although you get the feeling they used the sale as more of a way to clean out closets than make serious money. Pat held up some silver reindeer Christmas stocking holders for my inspection. "If you see something and the price isn't right we'll give it to you," she says.

It's hard to dicker with that kind of philosophy. I didn't need any more reindeer in my house, but I did walk away with a package of ten sharpies for a buck. What a day! As I snooped around all the booths, I also pondered taking home some fishing poles and felt happy that Evelyn finally reeled in her big fish: Georgia's largest yard sale.

"I feel like with the momentum we have going, it's contagious," she explains. "To me, it's like the Cherry Blossom festival. It started small with a lot of hard work and vision and now it's internationally known and I'm hoping this yard sale can blossom into something like that."

Hours/Seasons: Evelyn says this event will always happen the second weekend in March. They even checked with the Weather Bureau in Washington DC to make sure the weather may cooperate. It seems that historically we seem to get a good bit of rain the first weekend in March, but things clear up the second weekend. Now, of course Mother Nature tends to have a mind of her own, but Evelyn likes the odds.

Phone: (912) 375 5035

Website: www.goldenislesparkway.org

Extras: This runs from 1-75 in Perry all the way to 1-95 in Brunswick. It goes through the following areas: Hawkinsville, Cochran, Eastman, McRae, Hazelhurst, Baxley, and Jesup. You can pay $25.00 for an official spot along the route. Evelyn thinks so far she's got about 500 vendors and another 500 people just setting up in their garages or out on the lawn.

Pat's got stocking holders for sale.

Phillip with dogs to go.

Guy slopping around
in the volleyball tournament.

Battle of Byron

I've got to admit when I first heard about the Battle of Byron I thought it revolved around a band competition. I only had about half the equation right. The Battle of Byron is an all-out afternoon of fun centered on some classic competitions, great food, and lots of bragging rights for the year.

You can spend the day sitting on the sidelines watching folks fling themselves into everything from pie goo to sloppy knee deep Georgia red clay, or you can sign up for the fun yourself. Proud parents look on with video cameras as the karate club puts on demonstrations and cheerleaders will sell you snow cones with a smile. Firemen bring out the trucks for a wild ride through town and vendors peddle marshmallow guns to the kids. You can try your luck at a cakewalk, sit down for a little face painting, or purchase a few daylilies to take back home. This happens every year as a way for the tiny town to make money for their various service clubs, but like everything this festival evolved through the years.

Frances McDaniel spearheaded this event that began back in the seventies. "It was back when George Busbee was governor and, through the Department of Community Affairs, towns were encouraged to raise their own money rather than ask for grant dollars," she recalled. "So we had a competition with other cities our size and we won," she says.

McDaniel says that first year Byron earned enough money to give the downtown a fresh coat of paint, put up a basketball goal, and even lure Dr. James Livingston to town (The doctor still calls Byron home.).

The games between the cities throughout the state faded by the wayside, and actually the Battle of Byron did take a hiatus for a good many years. But the Battle is back, and McDaniel says it's the main fundraiser in town. "Well, the Masons are selling sausages; the Lions Club's selling lemonade and their famous brooms; the firemen get the money from the mud volleyball," she explains. And, yes, she did say *mud* volleyball. The red-clay, sopping-wet court is the highlight of the day as various teams step up to slosh, serve, and slime their way to victory. These men and women pay forty bucks a team or ten bucks a person for the right to act like muddy pigs in a pit, and I gotta say, as I tried to shoot pictures and keep my camera lens clean I really wanted to get in there with them and dive headfirst into a soft warm vat of the notorious Georgia earth. The firemen set the course and after every game they pump up the pressure in their water hoses and give the contestants a much-needed shower!

Phillip Shannon used to play in the volleyball tournament, but now he's a bit older and serves up ribs and chicken plates for a church called Allen Temple. "When it all began, we held the title for the first five years," he bragged. "They added the mud later on and, whew, after that mud you gotta wash up and that takes time away from other events!"

Shannon's got kids of his own now, cute little ones that ask Dad for money to go off and find treasures in the neighborhood streets. The Byron guy figures he's seeing everything come full circle. "This is a chance to give back to the community and mingle with people that you wouldn't normally see on a Saturday," he says. "I see kids and their parents from back then. As a matter of fact, I am one of the parents."

Don't be surprised to pull into town and see people wearing t-shirts that say, "I love Bob." "People say, 'Who is Bob?'" McDaniel says, chuckling. BoB stands for Battle of Byron, and for this tiny town to keep alive a tradition that fills the coffers of community groups for the year, well, you'll walk away loving Bob, too!

Directions: From Macon, take I-75 South to the exit 149 and take a right off the ramp. Go about a quarter of a mile and follow the signs to Main Street.

Hours/Seasons: The Battle of Byron happens the first Saturday in May. They've recently added a pre-event that happens the last Saturday in April; it's usually something like a concert or a dance.

Phone: (478) 956-2409

Website: www.byronga.com

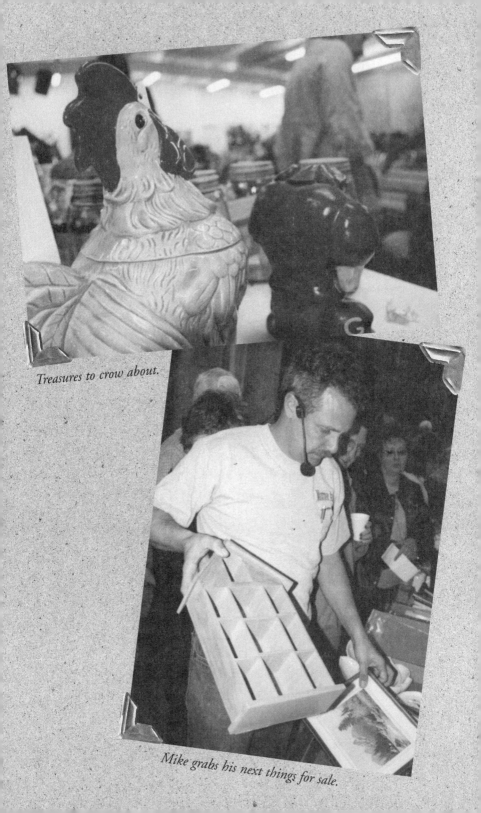

Treasures to crow about.

Mike grabs his next things for sale.

Montrose Auction

A lot of folks look forward to the end of the week to go out and
have a good time, but if you're the sort who likes to treasure
hunt, aim for Tuesdays in the tiny town of Montrose to find some
fun. Every other week a couple of guys open up their big blue warehouse that sits next to a cotton field to hold the Montrose Auction,
and for some it's the hit of the week. "This is the thing in Montrose
to come and visit," says Pam Frantz. Pam doesn't bid much; she
dragged 6000 pounds of personal belongings from California to
Georgia when she moved here, but she likes the auction atmosphere.
"They say there are no friends at an auction, but nobody gets angry
about anything," she explains.

They may not get angry, but they do take this stuff seriously.
The Tuesday bidding gets going about 6:30 P.M. I showed up around
five, but plenty of folks beat me through the door already working
out a game plan. They pilfered through the old pots and pans, sized
up the shot glasses...and fluttered around the furniture.

The bigger stuff sits on a stage that runs the length of the room.
There you might see old farm equipment, a bicycle looking for a
rider, a naked mannequin, chairs, planters, tables, and cabinets.

Sitting on four huge tables sits boxes and boxes of well junk.
They're called box lots and you might find anything from some old
45s to a painted birdhouse to an old coupon for Coca Cola. (I did
walk away with a winning bid on the Coca Cola coupon.) Rusted
car license plates share space with boxed up fishing tackle, a passel of
postcards, or some of Grandma's old china. And it's those box lots
that really draw the early scrutiny. Mike Ivie pointed out the people
clumping around the mystery assortments. "Look out there. Where

are the people? They're all around the box lots. They're digging out there, they love to find what's inside," he says with a smile.

Ivie owns part of the place. He used to come here for fun, but now he's submerged in the daily nuts and bolts of selling, even when it comes to selling nuts and bolts and whatever else comes along. "We've gone as far as Texas and New Hampshire to pick up stuff," he says. They pick up estate sales and sell a bunch of lots on consignment, which means you never know what you'll get to bid on when you come to town. "If you're saying 'I want a dresser,' you may have to come three or four times before you find one. Every week's going to be something different."

But when you find that dresser, ah, that's when the real talent comes in. I've got to admit I haven't shouted my way through many auctions before and I think it's not really an atmosphere for my personality. Here's what I mean. You have to be willing to part with money fast. Whether it's a dollar or a few hundred Benjamins, this is definitely an activity for quick thinkers.

The box lots go up on the chopping block first. Even though there are plenty of places to sit, folks crowd in like sardines around Mike; he's right in the middle of things, raising each box, describing it's contents, and looking for a bid. It's claustrophobic. Things disappear in seconds with people wondering what castoff comes next. And the bidding can get boisterous. "We start the box lots off at five dollars. If we can't get it, we add in another box. But a box has gone all the way up to $200 before."

The boxes are popular but so is history. And since a lot of this stuff comes out of folks' houses, the really interesting pieces up the ante. "We sold a pine cupboard out of Juliette dated 1864," explains Mike, "that brought in $2500 because it was a Georgia piece."

A piece of Peach state history can get the blood boiling because, even though this is the genteel South, there is a bit of competitiveness when it comes to winning. "Sometimes you can get caught up in it. You get determined saying 'I'm going to get it.'" Kathryn Dillashaw made the trip to Montrose for seven years for one reason: "Once you get it in your blood, you're hooked!"

Directions: Montrose is about halfway between Macon and Dublin off Interstate 16. From Macon motor on down I-16 West, until you see exit 32. At the top of the ramp, hang a left onto Georgia Highway 112E. Go about 1 mile till you see US80 and take a right. Go about 5 miles and that will bring you into the tiny town of Montrose. Look for the sign Montrose Auction. Take a left on Second Street and go two blocks till you see the big blue building.

Hours: Every other Tuesday night, the guys have the scratch-and-dent auction. One Friday night a month, they bring out the spiffy stuff for the antique auction. You'll find a lot more furniture and higher-end items on those nights. Check the website for specific dates and times.

Phone: (478) 376-4559

Website: www.montroseauction.com

Extras: The Montrose Auction is computerized, which means if you want to bid on something and leave you can just walk up to the window and check out.

Gerry in front of Henry's of Bolingbroke.

Town of Bolingbroke

In the South, antiquing is a sport, a weekend pastime if you will. And there is no better place to hunt for treasure than in the tiny town of Bolingbroke, Georgia. It's a small friendly place. The strip doesn't run more than a couple of miles, and even the town's gas station doubles as a country store. Along either side of a railroad track sit quaint little places to explore shop and eat.

"This is Mayberry. I sit on the front porch and watch the train go by, I just like it!" says Gerry Hailes. Gerry doesn't look like Aunt Bea but she does possess a lot of Southern charm. This stylish woman and her daughters have an antique space at Henry's of Bolingbroke. "I had an antique shop in Macon and sold it. My daughters came to me about six years ago and said, 'Why don't we get back into this?'" And so they did. Their room is one of twelve spaces in the co-op and you never know what you'll find. A good many metal things sit on the front porch, planters and garden art, inside you may find Mahjong boards and everything from pins to paintings. "You never know what people want, strange things," Gerry says. "We're selling a look that's old or gently used."

As you nibble on the key lime straws sitting out, make sure you take time to notice the house. It's an attraction in itself. "There is not one level floorboard in here that you can tell," Gerry explains.

Henry's is rustic yet modern. The downstairs even has exposed brick. "Three years ago we had some visitors in here from France and this was their favorite place," Gerry says.

Another favorite is Twila Faye's Tea Room. After a morning or afternoon of shopping, you're going to need some food. Twila and

Mike Dunlap got you covered. The main room is small and intimate with little tables dotting a colorful area. It all faces a giant polished wood soda bar in the front. Forget cell phones—an authentic phone booth from 1946 sits in the corner and it still works!

I believe in eating dessert first, so I ordered a vanilla milkshake as an appetizer. I could've gone all wild and crazy and sucked down an almond amaretto flavor, but vanilla is my favorite and I wanted to see what Mike could come up with. He does more of the ice cream and desserts while Twila invents the wonderful main entrées in the back, but we'll get to more of that later. Mike served one of the best vanilla milkshakes I've ever had. The main portion came in a typical milkshake glass, but then I also got the leftovers in a tall frosty metal cup. I love that! The milkshakes are blended and then blended and then blended. I didn't come across any icy chunks and it had a wonderful flavor.

Twila sold me on the house specialty for lunch. "I love the chicken salad, I do," she says. I loved it too, but looked forward to my next trip to check out the chicken, broccoli, and rice casserole or the Tea Room Delight, which comes with marinated veggies, glazed fruit, and nut bread served with a cream cheese filling.

After the milkshake, I had to wave off dessert, but Twila filled me in. "A lot of the cake recipes came from my mom. They're all homemade. My favorite is the key lime cake and the pecan cake. Nobody else makes it." Mike chimed in, "Yeah, she stays busy." I guess so since there are about fifteen cakes on the menu and that's only if you don't want a phosphate, ice cream sundae, or cream puff to top off your meal.

After such an experience, you're going to want to walk around more of the shops to work off the meal, but don't get too impatient to leave town. There is also a wonderful garden shop towards the northern end of town with all kinds of neat blooming things looking for a new home in your garden.

Now I've watched the *Andy Griffith Show*, but I think Mayberry's got nothing over the quaint town of Bolingbroke.

Directions: Just head up I-75 North until I-475 North splits off. Take I-475 and just out of Macon you'll see the exit sign for Bolingbroke (exit 15). Hang a left off the ramp and follow the windy roads into town.

From Macon, just take US Highway 41 (Vineville Avenue) north and you'll find yourself in the tiny burg.

Phone: Henry's of Bolingbroke, (478) 992-9878

Twila Faye's Tea Room and Soda Shop, (478) 994-0031

Extras: Twila's also does catering and they have a back room for bigger parties. Every Christmas the town does put on a big parade. You can go check that out and then mosey on over to the post office to mail off your holiday gifts. Gerry says it's the best-kept secret because they rarely have a line.

You can make yourself at home at the General Store.

Glenn and Katherine share a laugh.

The General Store

"If this isn't like Mayberry, than I don't know what is." Thirty-seven-year-old Glenn Johnson's got a good idea about life in Sparta since he's called it home since he ran the streets as a boy. Now as an adult in the modern world, he's a successful sales rep for the CBS television station in Macon. But every weekend he gets in touch with his past by opening up the General Store on Saturdays.

The pine-sided building first came to life in the 1880s (way before Glenn's time). The Cross family owned and operated this mainstay of the town up until 1945, but then, Glenn says, the General Store became generally forgotten. "In 1962, the Bank of Hancock bought the lot, and the bank didn't want the store, so they moved it next door into a backyard," explains Glenn. Years later Mrs. Katherine Hollis played her hand in history. The fashionable eighty-five-year old who doesn't look a day over sixty told the story with a twinkle in her eye. "Well it was covered in tin. Oh, it looked very black like it could never open its doors." Katherine's husband owned the bank that eventually took over the building. He didn't want it. As a matter of fact, the plan was to bulldoze the place for the timber, but Katherine wouldn't hear of it. "I thought too much of it to tear it down. Just look at this heart pine; it's at least a hundred if not more years old," she says.

Well, just about this time, Glenn had found himself a nice little side business of estate liquidations. The two parties struck up a deal. "The bank said you can have it if you'll move it and restore it." And that's exactly what he did. The new General Store opened in 2002 and it still serves as the mainstay in town. Katherine says she's always dropping by for a visit. "I come by every Saturday. It's just a place to hang out, see friends, and compare recipes."

For those who don't like to cook, Glenn's grandma provides quite a few sweet treats. You can buy cheese straws and lemon, coconut, or chocolate pies and cakes. But you've got to get there early. The weekend I dropped in three of granny's goods were already gone.

Oh well, they still had a jarful of penny candy, sodas for a quarter, and all kinds of stuff. You will have a different experience every time because of Glenn's scavenger hunts. I did pick up an old Soperton Coca Cola bottle. (Glenn's got a collection upstairs.) Dishes, salt and pepper shakers, books, vases, couches, rugs, lamps, hats, model cars, you name it and you might be able to find it on any given weekend.

But what makes this place more than just an antique stop is the fact that folks still use it as a general store. "That's the funny thing about it. There is still a need for this place," Glenn says.

Sparta is a small town and you won't find a mall for miles. So Glenn stocks lawn mowers, washers and dryers, mattresses, stoves, and daybeds. "You know we started with small stuff and people would say, 'Could you get so and so for me?' and then it just grew."

Or maybe the General Store just came back to life!

Directions: From Macon Take Highway 22 to Milledgeville. Go through downtown Milledgeville and stay straight on Highway 22 for 19 miles. As you enter Sparta go through that downtown (It's pretty small stay alert!). As you pass through the second red light, you'll see the Golden Pantry and Amoco. Turn left on Elm Street. Go down one block at the four way, The

General Store will be on your left. It sits at the corner of Hamilton
Street and Powelton Avenue.

Hours: The General Store is open every Saturday from 9:00
A.M. to 5:00 P.M. They also open up the first Friday of every
month.

Phone: As funny as it sounds in this day and age, they do not
have a phone. As Glenn put it, they wouldn't get to help anyone
because they'd be on the phone all day!

Website: You've gotta be kidding! They don't even have a
phone!

Jeannette and June.

British goodies on the shelf.

The British Pantry

I love the way Brits speak…but sometimes you've got to question how they name their food. The British Pantry in Warner Robins in no exception: you can pop in and pick up everything from bloater paste to blood sausage!

Now before you turn up your American nose, this place is definitely worth checking out. Everything is authentic from England, including the people. "We married GIs and came over when we were young and foolish." June Cox works the counter at the Pantry. If you don't buy a thing, just sit and talk with her for a few laughs and that wonderful accent. The owner of the shop Jeannette Francis described her friend as "talking the hiney off a horse!"

June is pushing seventy, but Jeannette convinced her to go back to work. "We wanted Brit girls in here—makes it more authentic," June says with a twinkle in her eye.

June is a hoot, but Jeannette, who hails from Berlin, brought this project all together, and she did it out of necessity. "My parents passed and I knew I wasn't going to go home as much." June piped in, "Had to buy your chocolate from somewhere."

The shop is as warm and inviting as a piece of chocolate. A table sits in the corner for afternoon tea, curtains hang on the windows, and soft blue tile lie on the floor. It's open and friendly and airy.

As an American you can identify most items, but they've often got a distinct oversea's flair. For instance, Heinz makes baked beans but they sit in a bright turquoise can. "Our baked beans are different than yours," Jeannette explains. "They're like bullets, harder with a sweeter taste."

Two things are a staple in the English diet: tea, which the store carries twenty different kinds, and gravy. "We like Bistro. They're gravy granules and you'll never have lumpy gravy again," says Jeannette. These guys eat gravy like we drink water. They pour it all over shepherd's pie, Yorkshire pudding, and of course toad in a hole (See recipe on next page.).

But the thing that almost made me run out into the street screaming is quite a delicacy in England. "We call it blood pudding," explains June. "That's congealed blood with fat in it."

"It's good if it's hot for breakfast," added Jeannette.

After that explanation, I needed a drink. The girls quickly opened the cooler and handed me a Shandy. After making sure it didn't have any blood in it, I took a sip and *Wow!* It's a mixture of beer and lemonade and it's tasty! "Kids would drink it in pubs," Jeannette says. But she went on to explain, "Now, you offer a good ole beer drinker a Shandy, he'll say, 'You're not ruining my beer.' But I like it."

The Brits have a section of fine china complete with teapots and cups, but if roughing it is more you're style they just rolled out a line of picnic baskets. Seems folks overseas will use any excuse to eat and drink outside. "We have in London piano in the park. We go around the lake and picnic," June recalled. "It would be nice around here, but the mosquitoes have a say on most things in Georgia."

Well they've got a point there, but after all every culture has its quirks!

Address: 100 Houston Lake Boulevard, Warner Robins, Georgia

Directions: From Macon, take I-75 South to exit 146. Turn left off the exit and drive about 2 miles. At the fourth light (with Eckerd's on your left), turn left onto Houston Lake Boulevard and then a right into the strip mall at the first light. The Union Jack will be flying if the British Pantry is open.

Hours: Monday–Saturday, 10:00 A.M.–6:00 P.M.

Phone: (478) 953-4009

Website: These guys say a website is in the works.

Extras: You can sign up for the British Pantry newsletter called *Pantry Patter* (It means to gossip.). June says just don't compare their British spelling to our American spelling. You can also get stuff by mail order and soon through a website.

Toad in the Hole

Batter: 4 ounces flour
1/2 tsp salt
1/4 pint milk
1/4 pint water
1 egg

Mix all together and beat until smooth. Leave batter to stand for at least thirty minutes.

1lb sausages

Place sausages in hot fat and put in oven for five minutes. Pour batter over the sausages and cook for forty minutes until a golden brown.

Serve with gravy, peas, and potatoes.

Bill's happy when he's behind the wheel.

The Generation Gap

Bill Bonbrake has one frustration in his life. It seems folks seem to wander right into his office in the middle of working hours. But if you saw his working area you might understand. You see inside the Generation Gap Antique Car Museum and Store... Bill does business right in the middle of a Knoxville Transit Commission Trolley. "This was sitting in the impound lot. I just rolled it in here and it became my office," he says.

And that's how things work in this place billed as Georgia's second best free attraction. (The Museum of Aviation gets top billing and you can find that in the first *Cotton, Cornbread, and Conversations!*) Anyway, the Generation Gap is a large warehouse and at any given time you'll see about thirty vintage cars lined up. You can walk around and enjoy the scenery for free and if the mood hits just pull out the old checkbook and take one home with you.

The history of how Bonbrake got to this point is as interesting as a yellow 1970 Mach 1 Mustang (which was for sale the day I stopped by). "As a little kid in Chicago my dad and uncle raced cars and boats," says Bill. Well, when the kid with the speedster in his blood grew up, he started working with Minnie Pearl (yup, *the* Minnie Pearl). Minnie had a series of restaurants that didn't fare as well as her country music. So Bonbrake went about liquidating those stores and that's how he learned the fine art of buying and selling. But eventually that led to buying and selling what he really loved: old cars.

He also loves the fact that he's created a small town museum with the cars center stage. When you walk around the Generation

Gap, you can see the town barber shop, the jail, and city hall. An authentic 1800s tanker sits under the facade of an old gas station. The whole thing lays out the road for a trip down memory lane, and Bonbrake says folks are always asking if they can spend all afternoon taking pictures. He says put it in gear and go.

"People always come in here and tell me stories of the cars they had. And then you get in the experts. Those guys are a hoot; they'll sit down and tell me everything," Bonbrake explains. Can you blame them? After all, most of the thirty cars that are present at any given time are the best conversation pieces. Take for example the purple and white Wild Hog Curtis Turner 1956 Ford Racecar. Turner "just dominated Daytona in that car," Bonbrake recalled.

So if you want to get inside the driver's seat, head on over to the Generation Gap. But do Bill a favor and knock before you ask to see the office!

Directions: Going south on I-75 from Macon, take a right off exit 149 in Byron, Georgia. It's right behind the Big Peach Antique Store.

Hours: Monday–Friday, 8:30 A.M.–5:30 P.M.; Saturday, 8:30 A.M.–1:00 P.M.

Phone: (478) 956-2678

Website: www.generationgap.com

Prices: Completely free so go in and spend as much time as you like looking around.

Racing car from the fifties.

Inside the Generation Gap.

Brother Callistus looks out over one of the gardens.

Inside the monastery.

Bonsai Monks at the Monastery of the Holy Spirit

Conyers is kind of stretching the borders for a book on Central Georgia, but when I head about a group of monks who grow bonsais I knew I had to make the trip. What I found is a place to find beautiful plants, a cavernous religious store complete with homemade fudge (also lovingly made by the monks), and a retreat where you are not allowed cell phones, televisions, or, if you choose, even the clatter of conversations.

A group of forty-five monks live on the spacious grounds. The Monastery of the Holy Spirit is a Roman Catholic order and the men take a vow of silence. It's a pretty strict promise, but the monks do have to make a living so some communicate with the guests and visitors.

When you first drive up, you'll realize you've found a pretty special peaceful place. The driveway is lined with thick and stately magnolias giving way to a parking lot with the store and bonsai sitting right out front.

Brother Callistus spent the day with me and gave me the tour. We started in the area that originally prompted the trip: the bonsai garden. The trees have a special place in the lush green nursery that also includes a huge variety of herbs and other plants. The bonsais range in maturity from brand new to hundreds of years old. You'll find youpon hollies, junipers, and boxwoods. Brother Callistus pointed out a special ficus retusa. It has a place of prominence because it was coaxed along by the man who started the Bonsai program:

Father Paul Bourne. This loving man with a reputation that spanned the country died quite a few years back, but the monks and a few volunteers have kept his passion alive and growing.

The monks feel passionately about everything that happens on their land. They are an order full of tradition and history. They are actually called the Cistercian monks or the Trapists. "The monks came in 1944 and when they got here they built a temporary farm-house and a wooden monastery," Brother Callistus explains. They spent the next fifteen years in those living quarters working on the church that you can visit today. And when you think about it, this was quite a feat because the church is mammoth, cavernous, and majestic. "It was built before heavy machinery and equipment," Brother Callistus says with amazement in his eyes.

The steeple is simple yet ornate. As you walk in to the impressive building, you see a huge open sanctuary with wooden pews and stained glass that, depending on the time of the day, showers the inside with reds blues and yellow light. "It's gothic architecture. The design is a typical design from Europe in the Middle Ages," Brother Callistus says.

The stone floor is dissected down the middle of the walkway by two wooden boxes running parallel to each other. This is where the Brothers sit at every mass and chant. "We've been chanting for 2000 years.... Basically, we sing, chant, they mean the same thing."

Mass occurs five times a day in the sanctuary and people that stay on the grounds for a retreat don't have too far to walk. It's another aspect of this experience the monks offer. For a nominal fee, you can spend the night in very basic quarter at the monastery retreat house. You won't find any telephones in the room and they ask that you keep conversation to a minimum. Brother Callistus says the monks only come by if they're called upon for spiritual guidance or confession. Meals come out piping hot from the kitchen and although the food is quite tasty you won't find folks shouting out culinary compliments because the dining room is supposed to be silent, too.

For a person like myself, it might be hard not to talk and concentrate on reflection and spiritual issues, but things get easier when you find out you can stroll the beautiful woodsy trails all over the property. You may even find yourself down by the lake, down with the ducks watching an early evening sunset.

No matter if you go for the bonsais, the abbey store, or to visit the men full of history chanting their praises to heaven, travel to the monks' land in Conyers. No doubt you'll walk away with some sort of gift from God.

Directions: From Macon, travel north on I-75 and turn left onto Highway 155 at exit 216. Turn right onto Highway 20 and left onto Highway 212 which is Browns Mill Road. Immediately after turning left onto Highway 212 you must turn left again to stay on 212. The monastery entrance will be on your right.

Phone: (770) 483-8705; monastery retreat house (770) 760-0959; abbey store 1-800-592-5203

Website: www.trappist.net (This is the main page but you can link to the Abbey store and the bonsai page off of this address.)

Extras: Mass is every day at 4:00 A.M. and 7:00 A.M.; midday prayer is at 12:00 P.M., 5:30 P.M., and 7:30 P.M. The retreat house holds sixty people and reservations are made months ahead of time. The monks suggest a donation of at least $50.00 a night. And if you like fudge, make sure you stop by the abbey store. Along with all kinds of religious items, monastic products, and reference books, you'll find containers of fudge. They have dozens of flavors, but the monks told me they put 7 pounds of peanut butter for every 30 pounds of fudge! (That's only for the peanut butter flavor of course!)

Paul singing on stage.

Couples on the dance floor.

Ole Clinton Opry

It took fifty years for Paul Moncrief to reclaim his voice in the world, but now he's built a stage for one of his passions in life. It's a place where everyone's invited in on Friday nights to enjoy gospel, country and a little bluegrass music.

Paul owns, runs, and shares the stage belting out tunes at the Ole Clinton Opry. Folks file in every week without ever paying a cover charge (They do pass around a paint bucket for donations.). It's mostly an older crowd settling in the barn-like building listening to a song that will have them jumping up to hit the dance floor. Ceiling fans spin lazily around in the rafters while bright lights illuminate some good local bands from around the area. You can chomp down on a sausage dog popcorn or candy from the concession stand or sip on a hot cup of coffee.

Louise Hunnicutt is a regular; she says she can't help it: "When Friday afternoon comes you start getting ready, it's just good clean fun you get up and shake your leg a little bit."

Margaret and Louie Hartley dance so close you might think they're still courting, and in a way you'd be right on the money. He's ninety-two; she's seventy-nine and they're newlyweds. When the music starts kicking the couple with happy feet just can't help themselves. "He says, You ready to dance?'" explains Margaret with a twinkle in her eye. "I say, 'I reckon so.' We love gospel, but we're not too fond of bluegrass. You can't dance to that," she says.

Well the lineup is pretty diverse to make everyone happy. And Paul says when people do start tappin' their toes, it just makes him smile. "If the bands are doing something that causes motion in their bones, then let 'em dance," Paul exclaims.

This Opry was a long time coming for the guy who grew up in the Depression. Life threw him quite a few sour notes during his childhood. Paul's dad died of pneumonia when Paul was five so the little tyke found himself with adult responsibilities on the farm in Crisp County. "I had to go out plowin' the mule in the late thirties," he recalls. His sister had twenty-one years on her little brother. All grown up and married, she would drop by and bring a coveted treasure: a radio. "Sometimes she would bring it out there and we would listen to the Grand Ole Opry. That's all you had to listen to in the country," Paul says. The kid grew up singing along to all his favorites, guys like Roy Acuff and, later on, Ernest Tubb. The years passed and at the ripe old age of seventeen Paul married his sweetheart Lois who still sits by his side today. It's a funny thing sometimes how a man can trade in some of his childlike enthusiasm for a chance to make a living.

While Paul couldn't sing with all his responsibilities on the farm, he and his wife still liked music so they'd visit an opry in Powersville. There Paul found the courage one night to ask one of the bands if he could sing a little. They obliged and he hit the stage. "I told the crowd this was the first time I ever sung with live music behind me. I was nervous, but I liked it," Paul says.

He liked it so much he became a student of sorts, learning how an opry worked with lights and sound. "I figured Jones County needs this bad, so I did all the legal work and had to get my ducks in a row," he explains. Those ducks came together after he had the land, and he even had a building because for years Paul had a fleet of big rigs that hauled chicken feed. The businessman built a big warehouse to bring in two trucks at a time to change the oil and work on the engines. Today the trucks are gone but cars do fill up the parking lot every week with dozens of folks piling in for a positive pastime. You'll see bands on stage like Phoenix, Paul Gary and his Country Band, and Heaven's

Treasures. Paul's got a simple motto: "I won't ever do anything that I couldn't do if God walked through the doors."

Well, it seems God may have a front row seat and encourages the man who first found a gift as a young boy and now spreads the joy throughout Central Georgia.

Address: 215 Old Highway 18, Gray, Georgia

Directions: From Macon take Gray Highway (US Highway 129) towards Gray. When you see Old Clinton Barbeque (featured in the first *Cotton, Cornbread, and Conversations*), look for Green Settlement Road on the left. Make the turn, go one block, and make another left on Old 18. Go down about a half a mile and you can't miss the parking lot on your left.

Phone: (478) 986-6587

Hours: You will find folks on the mike every Friday night. They perform three one-hour shows from 7:00 P.M.–10:00 P.M.

Website: www.oleclintonopry.com

Extras: Remember it is a bit of an older crowd, Paul says little ones are more than welcome, but they've got to behave.

Lisa holding some sausage.

Inside Stripling's.

Stripling's General Store

If you really like sausage—and I'm talking about the real stuff not that bright red pre-packaged meat, but real right off-the-bone sausage—then there's one place in Central Georgia you've got to check out.

Stripling's General Store caught my eye one night as I was traveling to Albany for a football game and believe me sausage was the furthest thing from my mind. And you, too, might be lured in by the homey-looking country store looming on the side of a pretty sparse road. I went in looking for a Coke, I came out with a true regional find.

"Well, we call ourselves a butcher shop, convenience store, and gourmet shop. We do have kind of a weird mixture of things," says Lisa Harden. Lisa and her husband Ricky own and run the store. It all started with Ricky's family and a little tradition they had back on the farm. His uncle James Stripling tinkered and worked out his version of the perfect sausage. He even opened a store on the family property called the Sausage Kitchen. It didn't have nearly the variety of the current Stripling's; folks could only buy fresh pork and sausage. When James died, Ricky figured he was tired of farming and decided to keep James's pork passions alive.

Lisa says they've got a couple of secrets to their success: first, the meat. "It's nothing like you buy in the grocery store," she explains. "We kill [the hogs], clean them, and make the sausage. We still even use the casings. It's very labor intensive, but the meat seems to take the seasonings better."

She also explains they use the whole hog product and don't chuck in any preservatives or fillers. As for the labor-intensive part, well, they've got lots of help. Butchers mill around the store. Some of the guys are working on the sausage and others are in standby, waiting to help folks who step up to the massive meat counter. "Some folks say they don't know how to buy meat here," Lisa says. "At the store you may get five pork chops; here you walk up and say I need five pork chops to fry or grill." The guys in the white coats will actually talk to you about how thick you want those chops and the best way to make sure you get a tasty meal.

It's customer service from the olden days. You'll see thick slices of cheese wrapped up in Saran Wrap by the counter. Lisa says nothing is ever frozen and resold, and my favorite touch is when the guys wrap up your meat in that crisp, brown paper.

Along with the sausage and chops you can also pick up tenderloins, ribs, and they just started selling big chunks of country and sugar-cured hams. The beef jerky is real, too. It's thin, stringy, and delicious, but just remember this is the authentic stuff, so you'll have to position it back on your molars, chomp down, and give a good yank.

Now, for folks who don't let out a big squeal over sow or the other meaty products, Stripling's has plenty of other culinary treats to tempt your taste buds. Rows and rows of bottled, canned, and packaged items sit on the shelf. You can find everything from marinades to marmalades carrying the Stripling name. We're talking everything from chili to cobbler mixes. But one item sits close to Lisa's heart. "My mother always made mayhaw jelly," she recalls fondly. For those of you who wouldn't know a mayhaw if it came and pounced on your head, like me, Lisa explains that these are trees that grow wild in low-lying areas. "It looks like a crabapple that makes the jelly really sweet."

And here's a word to the wise, if you think some of this stuff may work well under the tree or in someone's stocking during December, you're not alone. "Two weeks before Christmas, we did 13,000 pounds of sausage," Lisa explains. "People will say, 'Wrap me up a hundred packages of sausage, two links to a pack.' They like to use it especially for the men who are hard to buy for."

Well, it's not hard to see how this place found its success, although the couple who had doubts about pinning their future on pigs has come a long way. "When we started here, we weren't sure if we could pay the rent," Lisa says. But now rent isn't a problem; they've even got plans to expand and both of them are as happy as pigs in mud.

Directions: Take 1-75 South from Macon. It's a bit down the road to exit 99, also called the Georgia Florida Parkway. Hang a right off the exit. Stripling's is about 10 miles up the road on your left. You can't miss it. Now that's to the Cordele location. They also have a Moultrie store located at 1401 West Boulevard.

Phone: Cordele, (229) 535-6561; Moultrie, (229) 985-4226

Website: www.striplings.com

Extras: One of the things these guys are known for is their stuffed pork chops. You might've guessed they're stuffed with sausage, and you can buy it mild, medium, or spicy.

Stripling's Sausage Balls

1 lb. medium Stripling's pan sausage	2 cups Bisquick
8 oz. Cheez Whiz	

Mix sausage and Cheez Whiz together. Gradually add Bisquick: you may need to mix with your hands to blend together well. Roll into balls and bake at 350 degrees approximately 25–30 minutes.

Easy Stripling's Sausage Casserole

1 lb. Stripling's pan sausage	8 oz. cheddar cheese, grated
6 slices of white bread, cubed	6–8 eggs, beaten
2 cups milk	1 tsp. dry mustard

Layer ingredients in a 13x9x2 inch casserole in the following order: bread cubes, cooked sausage, and cheese. Beat together eggs, milk, and dry mustard. Pour over layers. Cover with foil and refrigerate overnight. Bake at 350 degrees for forty-five minutes. Serves six to eight.

Tickets cost just 16 cents decades ago in Thomaston.

Malcolm outside the Ritz.

The Ritz Theatre

When's the last time you caught a movie? Chances are you watched the flick at a megaplex complete with vats of popcorn and drinks so big that you could swim a few laps in the cup. I'm not knocking it. I love those places, too, but the folks in Thomaston have a different experience. When they see a movie, they get the big ticket on the screen and a dose of history walking through the door.

The Ritz Theatre sits on the town square, right across from the picturesque courthouse and down the street from the English Café (featured in the first *Cotton, Cornbread, and Conversations*. I know, I know, shameless self-promotion). You can't miss The Ritz's big yellow and turquoise phoenix-like exterior touting the latest movie to come out. Yes, I said *movie*, as in one—one theatre, one screen, that's it.

It's not so bad because few towns in America have working theatres that date back decades. "The Ritz was built on the site of an old mule stable back in 1927," says Malcolm Neal. Malcolm and his wife Amy own and run the theatre and café. We'll get to the eats in a few seconds.

But as for the big screen, the outside boasts a Hollywood-like atmosphere with a walk of fame documenting famous Thomaston folks. There is one long, cylinder-shaped ticket office and when you walk inside you'll notice the black and white checkered floor. The screen if 40 feet wide and 18 feet high, just perfect for King Kong to frighten the audience sitting in comfy rocking chairs under a decorative tin roof. "We haven't changed any of the seating. The red chairs are the same model as in the White House screening room," Malcolm explains. Malcolm, who speaks with a wonderful English accent, and Amy, who is from the Philippines, left a good bit of the theatre alone when they came to town in 1997.

This couple has a bit of an interesting tale themselves. The two met in the television business and eventually married and refurbished an old theatre out in Las Vegas. "We gutted it out and sort of got it going again," Malcolm says. After ten years of snowy winters, the couple decided they didn't want a Western address anymore. "We started looking around in trade journals but only Southern states," Malcolm explains. "The Ritz was open at the time and it needed far less work than the one in New Mexico," Malcolm recalls.

But the Ritz did need a little TLC and, of course, a cash infusion. "The ceiling was in disrepair, hanging down. It was something people said should become a town treasure again," Malcolm says. So Malcolm made a trip just a couple doors down the sidewalk. "The Bank of Upson gambled on this guy from New Mexico. Being right next door, I guess they thought they could keep tabs on us," he says with a grin.

Proximity may have played a role, but Malcolm possesses the charm of a gentleman with an accent that makes you want to sit and talk for a while.

So the Neals got to work and the town got to remembering that special movie house on the square. "Many people come in and say, 'I used to work here,' or 'I met my boyfriend or girlfriend here,'" Malcolm says fondly. "One woman even said, 'I married the first projectionist and we used to hang out up there.' Well, I don't know where the manager was," Malcolm says.

These days the managers and owners split their time between the screening room and the restaurant. It's a quaint little lunchtime café that doubles as the snack bar at night. "The previous owner started the café and Amy adapted quite a few recipes. Of course, steaks and fried foods are out of the question," Malcolm explains. So the couple concentrates on soups, salads, and sandwiches and, naturally, you can get some fresh, hot popcorn at movie time.

Many people in Central Georgia coo over the Ritz's chicken salad. And the café lays claim to their own bragging rights on Southern cuisine. "I don't know what's in it. She even keeps it a secret from me," Malcolm says.

Well, being the hard-nosed journalist I am, I pried the secrets out of Amy by merely asking her! "I use all homegrown herbs," she explains. "Lemon grass and rosemary and only trimmed fresh breast of chicken." There you have it, and for the folks with an adventurous palate, try the caramel popcorn sundae. And if you want to pay a couple extra bucks, you can eat the ice cream and even sip on a Cappuccino upstairs during the flick.

Writing about this adventure I can't help thinking about the parallels between *Field of Dreams* and the Ritz. The Neal's rebuilt it and the town of Thomaston has come—come to enjoy this silver screen treasure.

The Ritz Theatre

Address: 114 S. Church Street, Thomaston (right on the square in downtown)
Phone: (706) 647-7022
Extras: To sit in the balcony where you can order from the café will cost you two dollars in addition to the admission ticket. The Ritz is oriented toward families, so you will rarely find an R-rated movie at the Ritz. And you never know what might pop up at the Ritz. They have an orchestra pit and dressing rooms, so shows like the *Regional Finals of the Colgate Country Showdown* regularly light up the stage.

The Ritz Café

Hours: Monday–Friday, 11:00 A.M.–2:00 P.M., dine-in or take-out.
Phone: (706) 647-5372

Example of how the prisoners had to live in during the Civil War.

Soldiers' graves at the national cemetery.

Andersonville

As I write this book our military troops still have very dangerous and deadly missions in Iraq and Afghanistan. And right off the bat, I want to say how much I appreciate what they're doing. Of course, for those of us who have never enlisted in the military, there's no way of knowing what it's like to face a war in another country. But here in Central Georgia, Andersonville gives you a small taste.

In 1864, during the Civil War, the Confederacy opened Andersonville as a prisoner of war camp. The land sits close to a rail line and it had water, but as fortunes declined for the Confederacy, the care of the prisoners became less and less of a priority. Maybe it's best described by one of the men who lived through the nightmare between the huge log walls, "Once inside, men exclaimed: Is this hell? Verily the masses of gaunt unnatural looking beings soot begrimed and clad in filthy tatters and that we saw stalking about inside this pen looked indeed as if they might belong to a world of last spirits." (W. B. Smith, 14th Infantry, October 9, 1864. On a plaque on the Andersonville Field).

The sheer numbers that passed through the camp compounded problems that led to thousands of men dying from scurvy, pneumonia, small pox, and dysentery. Out of 45,000 that were imprisoned on the Georgia red clay, 13,000 didn't make it. The ones that did survive had to deal with gangs called raiders who roamed the 26 acres terrorizing the troops looking for food and supplies.

Allan Marsh has spent the last thirteen years giving tours and telling people the stories of the past. He's a park ranger and he has his own opinions on why things failed in the fort. "The

Confederate staff was in a bad place at a bad time," he explains. "Two things led to Andersonville being horrendous. One was overcrowding because you had 32,000 at one time in a camp built for 10,000 and the other thing was a lack of logistical support. We're looking at the last fourteen months of the war and the Confederacy wasn't in the best shape, so a camp holding prisoners of war was low on the priority list."

Today you can roam the field where so many suffered 150 years ago. Tattered canvas material still flutters in the wind stretched over flimsy pine tree stakes used as tents and shelter. The small stream still flows through the land. But ironically a sign is posted not to drink the water. "The water is unfit to drink. Folks don't realize if you're going to drink any water coming out of the ground you need to boil it to be safe," Allen says.

Many of the men that died never left Andersonville. Thousands of graves from the Civil War sit row after perfect row in the national cemetery. It's a somber site. "It was a place of sadness, but at the same time your final resting place is here with 13,000 soldiers who died for their country," Allan says. The ranger recognizes the patriotic spirit that a lot of veterans carry close to their hearts. Now, such patriotism is honored here in another way: Andersonville is a working military cemetery. The park service took it over in 1920 and Allan estimates they have about 175 services a year.

Myra and Norman Barkel stopped to pay respects. Norman served in the Korean War. Myra's emotions came to the surface after seeing the graves. "It's so sad, the heartache caused by each of these deaths," she says. Norman has the outlook of a man who's lived through war: "We were just following orders. We did it blindly," he explains.

Just a couple hundred feet from where men endured such brutal hardship decades ago sits a museum built in tribute to the troops that never came home from war. The Prisoner of War Museum has significant artifacts and stories from Andersonville, but it also touches on every conflict and the atrocities men and women have had to endure. You'll see a tiger cage built out of bamboo. Men had to survive in the hard box during the Vietnam War. You'll hear interviews from the families of prisoners of war as they live through their own hell of not knowing what's going on with their loved ones. You can spend hours pouring over the artifacts, captions and stories from every conflict in American history.

People visit from all over the country. Allan says most folks find themselves drawn here for the national cemetery, but after leaving they have a deeper appreciation for what all our veterans have gone through. "It's hard for your emotions not to be touched when you go through a place like this," he says. It's true but maybe now more than ever we need to connect with a place like Andersonville to remember the men who suffered in the Civil War and not forget the men and women fighting today.

Directions: From Macon take I-75 south to exit 149 and take a left. This will lead you directly to Andersonville. The park is located 10 miles northeast of Americus on Georgia Highway 49.

Hours: The museum is open every day from 8:30 A.M. to 5:00 P.M. The Parks Service staff only takes off Thanksgiving, Christmas, and New Year's. The national cemetery is open every day from 8:00 A.M. to 5:00 P.M.

Phone: (229) 924-0343

Website: www.nps.gov/ande/

Extras: One of the big events Andersonville holds every year is the Annual Living History Weekend. Reenactments and scenarios throughout the day include the arrival of prisoners, inspection of the camp, and a guard drill. This event typically hits in March.

Kathy and Fannie outside the trolley.

Milledgeville Trolley Tour

Some may say Milledgeville is one of the most historic cities in the state. At one time it stood as the center of politics for Georgia; the governor lived on Clarke Street and legislators shaped the future just a few blocks down the road. Today, you can soak in the antebellum atmosphere by hopping on a trolley and taking a special tour that heads out every day.

The day I stopped by, clouds and rain threatened to pour in on a winter day, yet the trolley filled up with folks wanting to see the sights. Carmen Cunningham even rigged up the adventure for her friend Angela Prosser as a birthday gift. Angela just turned sixty-three and wanted to know a bit more about her hometown history: "Guys from the Pilot Club came and told us about the tour and I was so embarrassed I didn't know about it and I've lived here my whole life," she says.

So we all piled onto the spacious, bright red trolley. Inside you'll have no problems finding a seat on the smoothly polished benches. Fannie Robinson's manned the wheel for nine years, and as soon as she turns the key, tour guide Kathy Fuller goes into overdrive with information.

She told us how in 1803 legislators put a cry out for a new state capitol. It seems the Creek Indians owed a good bit of money that they couldn't pay at the time so they gave up some land. Governor John Milledge was in office at the time. Kathy explains that he sent out a party of men and told them to find good land. He had two stipulations: it had to sit west of the Oconee River and it had to have a good water supply. The men didn't let him down and they named the town after their leader.

Kathy held our attention until the trolley stopped at the first of three locations. Lockerly Hall headlined the trip ticket. (We do talk about Lockerly Arboretum in this book and this mansion sits on the same land. But you can only visit the building on the trolley tour not just by stopping by the gardens.)

Richard J. Nichols built the house in the early 1940s and named it Rose Hill because of the Cherokee roses that are nestled around the grounds. Kathy says that decades ago it had its own gas and power plant on the property and that's something even the governor's mansion didn't have back then. Five families owned the property through the years, but the Hatcher family changed the name to Lockerly Hall. And the name is about the only thing that's changed; when you walk in its like going back in time.

Inside you'll find a beautiful walnut railing lining the stairs. Kathy told an interesting story by the banister. It seems the end piece stood hollow and that's where the families back then kept the mortgage. "When they paid it off, they put a decorative finial on top to show the house was paid off," she explains. You may find wonderful decorations including old prints of George Washington and a mirror that found its way to Georgia from the Truman White House, but you won't find too many closets. Kathy came in with the answer. "They paid taxes by rooms, and a closet signified a room so that's why you see a lot of armoires."

The house oozes with charm. Just ask Carmen. "Most old homes look ominous but this looks like you could just move in and be happy."

Well, we couldn't move in. As a matter of fact, we had to move on to the next part of the adventure: the old capitol, which sits preserved on the campus of Georgia Military College.

Inside the trolley during a tour.

Construction crews finished the original project in 1807. Kathy says its one of the only gothic style capitols in the country. Fire became its biggest enemy, breaking out numerous times, but each time the town rallied and rebuilt the building.

Today, the senate chamber houses the GMC offices, but the house chamber still looks the way it did decades ago and during the tour Kathy couldn't resist sharing a quick history lesson: "Back then they didn't have telephones so people who wanted to influence legislators had to come and talk to them in this lobby. Guess what they were called?" she asked. "Lobbyists! And the name stuck!"

We got back on the train en route to the next place, but along the way Kathy threw out tidbits: Memory Hill Cemetery on Franklin Street is where Flannery O'Connor is buried and you'll find a grave for the famous train robber Wild Bill Miner, too. It's said Miner would politely ask for people's money before galloping away with the loot. Miner's actually in an unmarked grave, but the town still passes on his colorful history.

We wound up the morning at Saint Stevens Episcopal Church. The chapel with the big dark wood timbers went up in 1843 and they've had services almost every Sunday since then.

General Sherman did throw a wrench into things when he took a liking to the place back during the Civil War. Kathy says he burned the pews for firewood and housed his horses inside the building. "If you pull up the carpet, you can still see the horse scratches on the floor," she says.

Sherman's men didn't have too much respect for the little church either: they poured molasses on the organ.

Kathy told us a little girl by the name of Nylic didn't take too kindly to that. So, she wrote a letter to the head of the New York Life Insurance company because her dad worked for them and told the company president what happened. The company offered to pay for a new organ and the locals will tell you it helps make the Sunday services pretty special even today.

The tour only lasted two hours, but it seemed we could have spent the entire day listening to the fascinating tales of a town that once stood at the heart of Georgia life.

Directions: From Macon, follow Highway 49 (which is also Shurling Drive) north right through to Milledgeville. The convention and visitors bureau sits directly across the street from Georgia College and State University at 200 West Hancock Street.

Hours: The trolley runs Monday through Friday at 10:00 A.M. and Saturday at 2:00 P.M. All tours begin at the convention and visitors bureau.

Phone: (478) 452-4687; 1-800-653-1804

Website: www.milledgevillecvb.com

Cost: Ten dollars for adults and five dollars for kids ages six to sixteen.

Extras: During special times of the year, the trolley goes on special runs. In the spring, you can hop on board for a spring home and garden tour. Only the bravest ghouls take a ride in October for the Haunted Trolley Tour and in December don't forget about the Holiday Tour of Historic Homes.

There is a lot to see in Milledgeville, especially for history buffs. Be sure you check out the Old Governor's Mansion. The city's done a fantastic job refurbishing the giant house. The project cost $9 million and it really looks like it did back in the 1850s.

Memory Hill is also a wonderful old cemetery with a listing of where the town's most famous people are buried and a grid of where you can find the markers.

The stage curtain inside the opera house.

The Hawkinsville Opera House.

Hawkinsville Opera House

You may not think that culture comes often to a small town like Hawkinsville, but the Hawkinsville Opera House in Pulaski County has seen everything from vaudeville acts to pianist Jim Brickman grace the stage.

In 1907, back when the main roads through town had more dirt than asphalt, the town built a city hall and attached an ornate auditorium to the building. "They used the same architect who built the Grand [Opera House] in Macon and the Springer Theatre in Columbus," says Julie Stewart. She knows a lot about the place and she speaks with pride in her voice. And why not? She's put in a lot of sweat, elbow grease, and man-hours getting the opera house back to its old glory, but I'm getting a little ahead of myself.

Back in the early 1900s, folks would come from all around, including neighboring states, to either see a show or perform on its big stage. Nearly every weekend, the folks would fill up the 576 seats (They only have 382 now because the average audience member became physically larger and in one of the remodels they had to expand each seat by 4 inches!). Nellie Coley remembers a steady stream of good shows passing through. You see, back then performers traveled on a road show circuit. "This was the main drag from Augusta to Atlanta," she says, "so this was a stopping-off point. They would finesse [their act] here to be better at the other places."

The opera house really stood at center stage during its heyday, but old buildings need constant TLC and by the 1960s the opera house eventually looked more like a haunted house. It really started to go downhill when the city hall moved away. Luckily, some folks in town cared enough to save the venue from bulldozers. They figured the place needed a title and a little help from the government to ensure its safety for the future. So, in the late 1970s, they put together a group that would stage plays again. "They got money to fix the holes in the ceiling. After all, you've got to be in a building to show the state you want to preserve it," Julie says.

The group had a goal to hang a National Registry of Historic Places plaque on the front entranceway. And just like Lance Armstrong winning a Tour De France, each group chipped away to move the project forward until they got the job done. As a matter of fact, Julie's husband had a role in the production *Low and Behold* in 1982, which served as a springboard to get the wheels rolling again.

Today, Julie says she stays busy booking a performance almost every week. Marty Stewart, B. J. Thomas, and Chuck Leavell have stopped by. "I can't wait to get up in the morning because it's always something different," Julie says with a smile. "We rent it for beauty pageants and we even had a wedding from Las Vegas on stage." Now, that is a switch, but you gotta figure those folks from out West fell in love with the charm. When you walk in, you get a feeling of old and new at the same time. Soft-colored walls outline red comfy chairs that sit facing a huge stage with a curtain that depicts a country scene with rolling fields and a woman tending to sheep.

Ted Coleman's played the dulcimer in front of the decorative drapery. "Well, the curtain's a copy of the original," he says. "During the time the opera house sat empty, it rained on the old one." The University of Georgia Arts Department thought they could restore the curtain that billowed down from the rafters.

"They kept it for a year and couldn't repair it, but they made an exact duplication except it goes straight up and down. It doesn't roll," Ted explains.

If you really want to impress your friends when you go the Opera House, tell them the story of the safe that wouldn't stop rolling. "When they built the old bank at the corner, there was a vault, and they just rolled it down the hill because they had to get it out of the bank," Julie says. "It's still here."

Now, I personally didn't see this big black piece of history, but if you don't mind getting a little dusty you might get a glimpse. "You can still see it if you want to crawl underneath the opera house. They built right over it because they couldn't move it," Nellie says.

The safe along with the rest of the building seems in good hands these days. The city owns the title and the arts council leases it. Julie says it's not in business to make money but just make things a little more entertaining for people. And who knows? Maybe a hundred years down the road instead of Oliver Hardy they'll look back on that Vegas wedding and remember the good ole days that seem to emerge every week in Hawkinsville.

Address: 100 Lumpkin Street, Hawkinsville, Georgia
Directions: From Macon, take I-75 South to exit 135 (Marshallville/Perry). Take a left off the ramp and drive about 21 miles to Hawkinsville. When the road deadends in town, turn left and drive four blocks. You'll see the opera house at the intersection of Broad and Lumpkin streets.
Phone: (478) 783-1884
Website: www.hawkinsvilleoperahouse.com

A fisherman with his catch from the swamp.

A tree frog hides among his surroundings.

Bond Swamp

A couple years back a 300-pound alligator crawled out onto US Highway 247 during morning rush hour. Needless to say, his presence kind of upset folks and some couldn't figure out where the rowdy reptile came from. Well, the rangers showed up and pointed the big guy back home towards Bond Swamp.

Bond Swamp nestles right next to Bibb County. The 65,000 acres are only 6 miles outside of Macon running along the Ocmulgee River. A lot of folks helped to make this area accessible to the public, but it all started with a simple gift to Mercer University years ago. "Mrs. Mary Johnston Ray left a little over 5000 acres to the school and the US Fish and Wildlife service acquired it from them," Carolyn Johnson explains. Johnson is a ranger with the wildlife service and she says Mrs. Ray's house still sits across the street from the swamp.

Johnston made her donation back in 1979. The wildlife service got some help from the Nature Conservancy to buy more land and open it all up to the public. By 2000, hikers, fishermen, and hunters could walk the trails.

It's a beautiful area and Johnson says it even stays green in the winter because of the swampy atmosphere. You'll hear woodpeckers working the trees and see butterflies dancing along the trails. Squirrels scurry about their business while white-tailed deer try to stay out of sight. But keep in mind, this is nature up close and personal and Johnson says some folks come out to the wilderness not quite prepared for their experience. "If you don't bring bug spray in June you're not going to last," she says. "Some people say the mosquitoes are the size of hummingbirds!"

The bugs do hit hard and heavy in the summertime, but critters that crawl close to the ground call this place home, too. "Well, this is a swamp. You'll see a lot of snakes, but only a few are venomous," Johnson says.

You've got to take a cautiously optimistic attitude going into the area, especially down by the water. I love to fish, and Johnson says the water quality is good, so you can expect to pull out bream and bass, but the afternoon I visited, a snake did seem to want to make my company. He hung out about 20 feet away. I was pretty

Forest Trail.

sure he wasn't poisonous and he didn't bother me and I didn't bother him. And although I didn't catch any fish, I did get to photograph a tree frog, a rather large spider, a field mouse, and some curious turtles. I walked away with some exciting stories for an afternoon of not catching any fish and that's the magic of the swamp!

"It's neat that it's so close to the city," Johnson says. Right now, a lot of folks from Macon's industrial area visit at lunchtime and Johnson says the Middle Georgia College cross-country team trains on the trails.

So, if you want an experience that makes you feel like you've gone hundreds of miles away, deep into the woods, just skip right outside the city line to Bond Swamp. Oh, and tell that friendly little snake I said, "Hi."

Snake.

SUZANNE LAWLER

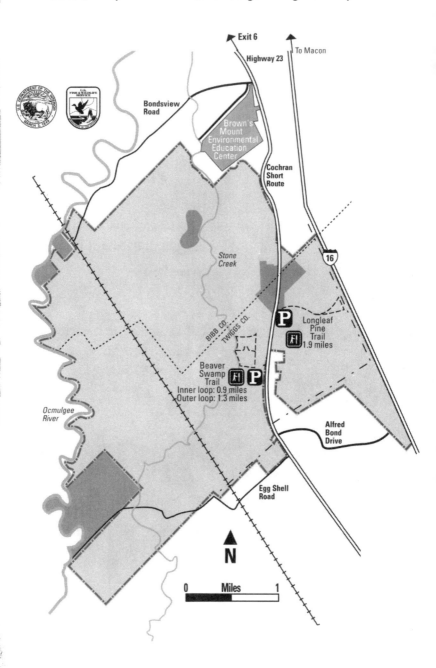

Directions: From Macon, take I-16 to exit 6. Take a right off the ramp and go about 4 miles down the road. You can access the swamp from three places. I went down by the Stone Creek Trails, but you will have to walk about a quarter of a mile or so to get down to the water. You can also use the Reid Station road which gives you access to drive right up to the edge of the bank. There is also a way in off Bond View Road, but Carolyn says it's not the easiest way to get down to the swamp.

Phone: (478) 986-5441

Hours/Seasons: Bond Swamp closes at sundown. Fishing season runs from March 15 to October 15. Bow season is in September. And the rangers do schedule three gun hunts a year when the swamp shuts down to other visitors.

Extras: You must have the proper state licenses when you fish or hunt on the land. Plus, boats are not allowed in the water. The trails are dog friendly but beware: you may run into a snake out there and your pal does have to stay on a leash. Bikes are not allowed on the trails and the swamp does not have any camping sites.

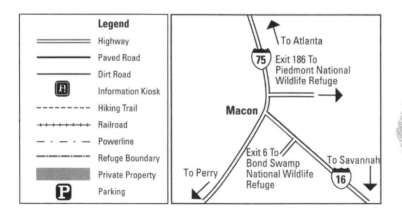

Legend
- Highway
- Paved Road
- Dirt Road
- Information Kiosk
- Hiking Trail
- Railroad
- Powerline
- Refuge Boundary
- Private Property
- Parking

To Atlanta
75 Exit 186 To Piedmont National Wildlife Refuge

Macon

Exit 6 To Bond Swamp National Wildlife Refuge
To Perry
To Savannah
16

Lynn and Mary.

Ladies having fun at Paintin' and Kiln Time.

Paintin' and Kiln Time

When you walk into Paintin' and Kiln time on Ingleside Avenue, you have to prepare for your imagination to go into overdrive—I'm talking slap shooting it into outer space. Here, you have so many options.

It's primarily a ceramics studio, but you can do everything from tiling your favorite photograph to creating a new necklace. When you walk into the bright yellow and blue atmosphere with happy bright lights, you get the feeling you're going to have some fun. All kinds of interesting objects line the walls just waiting for you to pluck them off the shelves and paint them. You can choose vases, pet bowls, utensil holders, soap dispensers plates, and the list goes on and on.

When I stopped by on a hoppin' Friday night, Jenny Allen had a seat with some of her pals paintin' some pretty cool stuff. "These are matching heels," she says, showing off her work. "They'll sit on my coffee table and one is going to hold the TV remote and the other is going to hold a cell phone. It's just fun. You can talk and laugh and even if you're bad at it its still fun," she says.

The thing is, it's hard to be bad at ceramics. Although, I gotta admit, with a pristinely white piece of work staring back at you, it may take a few minutes to know where to begin. But, Mary Gogul and Lynne Barta got you covered. "Probably 90 percent of people come in here and say, 'I'm not creative,' but you don't need to be," Lynne says. "It is like a big piece of a blank canvas," Mary chimes in, "so we try to have samples out so people can envision what it can look like. You can also draw with a marker or a pen—the marks fire out—or I'll go to the computer and print out clip art," she explains.

Mary and Lynn don't charge by the hour, they charge by the piece. So you can take your time perusing over paints like Leapin' Lizard, Blue Yonder, and Butter Me Up. Feel free to sit and pass the time away in the studio with soft music playing in the background. "I think a lot of people come in to relax. It's just a stress reliever," Lynne says. "We hear that all the time."

Lynn is an accomplished photographer and she's woven her love of the camera right into the studio. You can buy any of her prints that are displayed in the studio like a gallery of Central Georgia and beyond. Lynne knows that everyone has their favorite shot, so the women have started a mosaic photo class.

In a side room, you can put that 4x6 or 8x10 on a mount and then work in the pasty concrete concoction. "Some people think you have to take the picture apart," Lynne says. But actually you're just working the grout to make it appear the photo is tiled. It is a really neat affect and much more striking than putting something in a frame.

Recently, the women started offering another outlet for you to explore: glass fusing. With this technique you can make everything from your own original jewelry to contemporary coasters. Folks first have to take a class on glass cutting and then you're only limited by your imagination. You'll find all kinds of glass pieces to play with and even little confetti-like stuff called frit to lie into your masterpiece.

It's part of the charm and pizzazz that makes things always new and exciting at Paintin' and Kiln Time!

Directions: From I-75 South get off at exit 164 and turn left onto Hardeman Avenue. Go through five lights and turn left onto Corbin Avenue. Go to the next light, which is Ingleside Avenue, and Paintin' and Kiln Time is three doors down on the right.

Hours: Tuesday–Saturday. Hours vary by season, so call ahead.

Phone: (478) 738-9321

Website: www.paintinandkilntime.com

Prices: For the ceramics studio, when you pick a piece off the shelf just add half of that again for the time in the studio, all your paint, and the firing. So, if a piece is ten dollars, your total bill would run fifteen. The Mosaic photos and glass fusing have a variety of prices.

Extras: One popular feature is to buy a plate and take it to a party or wedding reception, get everyone to sign it, and bring it back for Mary and Lynn to fire in the Kiln as a gift. You can also get these guys to come to your office or home for a party. Lynne also offers photography classes periodically, and the last Friday of the month the women try to have a theme night.

Tobler Mill.

Bill has to release the water to make the meal.

Tobler Mill

B ill Browning's life changed forever when lightning struck him
one fall evening. I'm not kidding, it really happened. You see Bill
worked as a freelance crane-camera operator for ABC and one night
fate played the final down in his career. "It happened October 22,
1994, in a game between Alabama and Mississippi State," he recalls.
"It went through the headset and burned my ear out, and it took
about eight years out of my life." Bill had to retire at the age of fifty-
two, but these days that's quite young for a frisky man of Bill's
personality. So as he recovered, he reacquainted himself with his
favorite pastime of fly-fishing. "I fished a lot of smaller creeks and I
looked at this place several times, but the camp was all covered in
Kudzu," Bill explains.

That old, vine-filled camp on the river is today a beautiful working mill that Bill brought back to life. Before he put in the manual
labor though, he hit the history books "Well, the historical society in
Upson County goes back to 1825. James Hightower was the first tax-
payer on the mill," he says. "There was a town called Tobler, Georgia,
here up until 1915. It had houses, the mill, and two stores. That's the
last records I found of it, but it was pretty much the hub of activity
back then."

Connie's worn a wedding ring with Bill for forty-four years and
when he told her about his ideas of bringing the old mill back to life
she thought, "Okay, a weekend place." "I loved the water and I
thought we were going to build a cabin and have a little fishing. I
didn't think it would get to this magnitude," she says with a smile.

The mill itself is like a big majestic treehouse perfectly
positioned near the rushing water of the creek. Big windows let the
sunshine in to accentuate the history that Bill's carefully chronicled

on the wooden walls of the place. A huge water wheel helps him grind out corn just as they did decades ago.

When you visit the mill, the man who brought history back to life will detail every record he's found for you and let you look at all the black-and-white photos of men showing off their catches in front of the first mill. But the real treat comes when Bill decides to start grinding corn. Yup, this is a working mill complete with big stones that make sure every visitor walks away with a tasty souvenir. "Well, one day Bill says to me, 'I think we're going to grind corn,'" Connie remembers, "and I said, 'I don't have to grow the corn, do I?'"

Connie never had to grow a single green stalk, but she does her part in all of this by sharing a really good recipe for cornbread on the back of every bag of corn meal that walks out the door. Bill is the one who has to put in the hard work to make all this happen. He scoots out the back door and starts pushing levers to open the sluice on the back porch. It's a laborious yet simple operation. "I divert the water to run the wheel to grind the corn," Bill explains. The mammoth wheel starts to move under the weight of the water. "I got the two big stones from a guy in Bryon," Bill says. Those stones work together in a noisy process to make the ground product pop out into the bags.

The whole operation is really amazing and you don't know which part to watch first. A series of pulleys run like clockwork, moving on greased tracks as the lumbering process unfolds before your eyes. "The only way to turn it off is to take the water off of it," Bill chuckles. "It'll keep you busy once you get started now."

This whole dream-turned-reality is a process that has kept the former camera guy busy. He used to shoot plays that unfolded before his eyes, but now he's showing people history unfolding in the tiny town of Yatesville. "He's loved every minute of it. I'm glad he restored the mill," Connie says, sitting down to a slice of cornbread.

He's got a new project and a new sparkle in his eye, but as for the hobby that got him here in the first place... Well, let's just say those poles have collected a little dust. "I haven't fished to speak of in three years," Bill says, grinning.

Directions: From Macon, take Highway 74 west towards Thomaston. Just past the Upson County line, you will pass through Yatesville. The mill is in this small town just over the river and to your right.

Hours: Friday, Saturday, and Sunday, 11:00 A.M.–4:00 P.M.

Phone: (706) 472-3261

Website: www.toblermill.org

Prices: Bill will give you the complete tour of the place and even grind corn for you without asking for a dime, although donations aren't turned down.

Extras: Bill and Connie have started a tradition of having a Tobler Mill Arts and Crafts Festival in early April. They haven't settled on a permanent date, so check the website for further details.

Connie's Tobler Mill Cornbread

2 cups fresh-ground, (sifted) Tobler cornmeal	1 egg
1 cup self-rising flour	2 tsp. baking powder
1/2 cup sugar	1–1 1/4 cup of milk
	Approx. 1/4 cup of hot oil

Mix ingredients together. Heat the vegetable oil in a cast iron skillet. Pour a small amount of hot oil into the mixed cornmeal. Pour the cornmeal mixture into the skillet. Bake at 350 degrees until golden brown for thirty minutes. Enjoy!

Outside of Karsten-Denson downtown.

5 # 11.99

turf-type

TALL Fescue

GRASS seeds

You can buy grass seeds by the handful or by the bag.

Karsten-Denson

I have a really good friend who will not buy her tomato plants from anyone except the folks at Karsten-Denson. It's her annual spring pilgrimage to this downtown Macon hardware store to pick out the best looking little plants that sit on the sidewalk.

By definition, Karsten-Denson is a working hardware store, but nowadays in a world full of Wal-Marts and Home Depots (and I do like both those places), folks who walk in through the door of this humble place come in for the experience as much as for shopping.

If you only want one screw washer or nail, no problem. Just pick as many or as few as you want out of the bins. You'll find everything from birdhouses to boots, coolers to dog collars, spreaders to saws.

Roselyn and Frank Fountain made the trip in from McIntyre for their spring plantings, too. Frank figures he's going to lay down a couple hundred tomato plants this year, so he scoped out the Better Boys and the disease resistant Amelia 0800 series. "This store has a history. You can depend on what you get here," Frank says.

Johnny Davis owns the place and he spent time with the Fountains out on the sidewalk listening to their tomato tales. "The thing with this store is people can ask, 'Why did my plants die last year?' We try to have a little more knowledge," he explains.

Davis bought the store a few years back, but the history of Karsten Denson itself dates back to the 1920s. The current owner has records and receipts in an old filing cabinet that sits in the office. "Mr. Karsten started it. He moved down from Chicago, I think, in the early twenties and opened the store from scratch," Davis says. "He took on Denson as a junior partner." Denson eventually ran the place and it's had only a handful of keepers since then. Davis kind of fell into the position. "I was running an ACE Hardware for my brother in Gray, but I thought I would always like to have my own store. Then I heard about this through the grapevine," he says. "I had always heard about Karsten-Denson but I was raised in Gray, so we went to the feed and seed there. Several people advised me not to do it downtown, that this just wasn't a shopping destination any more. As a matter of fact, Saturdays are our slowest day. My wife even said, 'Are you sure you want to do this?'"

Davis did want to do it and he says he looks forward to coming to work every day, although he did make some changes. He moved out a lot of the higher-end pottery the store used to carry and brought in the basics. "I've put in a lot of new inventory. We sell a lot more hardware than we used to. Now, we're a hardware store with a little feed and seed on the side. It used to be the other way around." So nowadays you'll find toilets, light switches, and saws. And if you have critters running around, well, apparently it's a common problem. "Macon is full of rats and being close to the river we sell rat poison and we sell gobs of insecticides. It's unglamorous, but it's kept the business going."

The seed business may take a back seat to the stuff we need for everyday life, but walking through the door of this hardware store is worth it just to shove your hands into a vat of kernels that could one day produce tons of beans or squash. Large elephant ear bulbs sit out on the counter while a filing cabinet that looks like it uses the Dewey decimal system holds a vast variety of seeds. "We sell a couple of tons of seeds a year, but that's going out the door a couple of ounces or pounds at a time. The market is shrinking though. We are a different people than our parents' generation. People just don't buy 5 pounds of squash seed or a bag of pink eye purple hulls, and outside the south people don't grow that stuff at all," Davis says.

We may live life differently than our parents, but the spirit of our moms and dads still makes us stop by the old store to relive memories. "Not a day goes by that someone doesn't walk in and say, 'I came here with my granddaddy to buy chickens' or 'I came here on a Saturday and drove our buggy with a mule and went back and planted some seeds,'" Davis says.

The days of horse and buggy are over, but you can still buy chickens in the spring—seems those go right along with the canning supplies and the plastic owls for the garden. Davis is true to the hardware salesman, and although he realizes Karsten-Denson is an experience, he's never going to go overboard by selling brownies and postcards at the counter. "During Cherry Blossom, we have people come by because there just aren't many old hardware stores in business that's not a cutesy gift store. I guess I've got some gifts, but we're functional. We make money by selling what people need."

And in the purest sense that's why my friend figures she always needs to take another trip to Karsten-Denson for those little tomato plants.

Address: 536 Third Street, Macon, Georgia.

Directions: Karsten-Denson is located at 536 Third Street in downtown Macon.

Hours: Monday–Friday, 8:30 A.M.–5:30 P.M.

Phone: (478) 745-3306

Extras: Right around Easter you can actually buy ducks and chickens. Johnny also opened a second location in Ingleside Village at 2323 Ingleside Avenue. It's a little smaller than the downtown spot, but you'll still find plenty of hand tools, hardware, and tomato plants in the spring.

Henderson Village is a place to sit and relax.

The striking garden fountain.

Henderson Village

Heather Bradham is perplexed. "It still amazes me, people we meet every day…don't know about Henderson Village," she exclaims. Henderson Village is like an oasis in the burning sun of Central Georgia heat. Just off the interstate sits acres and acres of gorgeous gardens and shady cottages just beckoning for you to stop by and spend some time. Think of it as a luxurious Southern hideaway.

The place sits on 17 acres with another 3500 acres available for hunting trips complete with dogs and wagons. Heather runs the place now, but actually all of this started coming together years ago when a German man fell in love with a very Southern tradition. "When Bernhard Schneider was a kid, his aunt owned a small hotel and he would watch American movies," Heather explains. "He saw *Gone With the Wind* and fell in love with the South." Fortunately, Schneider made enough money in the electronics business to recreate his dream in Georgia. Back in the seventies, he started buying the land where the village sits today, and then a funny thing happened: the people in Henderson pitched in. "Well, Miss Dolly Newberry, who was a widow, offered to sell Schneider her house for the land. Mrs. Hodge, who was also a widow, sold him her house, too, and then Mr. Schneider figured, 'Maybe I could create a village,'" Heather explains. It takes a while to put together a dream, and a couple of decades did pass before Schneider really could open to visitors, but in the meantime, farmers in the area offered six cottages to add to the idea. Now, these cottages didn't come all nice and cute like they appear today. No, they came to the German entrepreneur in shambles, and he had to literally put them back together. The Langston House was the last structure to make it to the village and in order to buy this historic house with original 1838 hardwood floors Schneider had to add his own town car to the deal!

The Langston House now serves as a focal point in the village. Be prepared to sit down for a wonderful meal once you walk through the doors. We had stuffed mushrooms with a wonderful smoky flavor and gooey cheese and herbs bursting out of their crowns. Heather says they harvest frequently from the herb garden that flanks the kitchen.

This woman who grew up in South Carolina had a few ideas for the menu when she came on board as the general manager: "Well, I said to the head chef Alex, 'Let's put shrimp and grits on the menu,' and he said, 'Are you out of your mind? They won't sell.'" Heather says with a twinkle in her Southern eye, "We bet fifty dollars on it and people went crazy over them." Those grits are still a mainstay on the menu. I asked Heather what she did with the fifty bucks. "I didn't get the money," she answered. "Alex just said, 'You were right,' and that's better any day of the week."

The grits are wonderful. Big shrimp sit on a generous portion of the white creamy concoction. You get the idea this can't rank as healthy food, but that's okay. And since this is the kind of place to splurge, definitely opt for a dessert. I don't consider myself a chocoholic, but I think my favorite was the chocolate ganache cake. It had almost 2 inches of ganache and just a thin slice of cake—just the way I like it! The chefs also prepare a fantastic warm crème brulee and a delicious toffee cake with caramel sauce.

After such a meal, you'll immediately think about a nap or a good night's sleep. In keeping with the entirely relaxing atmosphere, whether you stay in a cottage or a suite in one of the houses, all of the rooms are done in soothing whites and yellows. Although Mr. Schneider only visits the property, he's left his mark in every room with a Schneider tower stereo for your enjoyment. Along with nightly turn down service and a handmade chocolate on your pillow, Heather also leaves a note in the room with a special message. And in the bathroom, you'll find one of two special tubs: ones with old-fashioned claw feet or ones with jets to work out those sore muscles from a day of horseback riding at the village. In the wintertime, feel free to turn on the working fireplaces, and if you want a bottle of wine to sit and enjoy on the front porch, no problem. It will be hand delivered.

In the morning, feel free to send the kids down to the barn to feed carrots and apples to the horses while you check out the garden greenery. You'll see hostas and hydrangeas, rosemary and roses. Henderson Village is wonderfully landscaped, so you can sit and relax in the herb, gazebo, or fountain gardens.

The fountain is quite ornate, with sculpted birds shooting out water that cascades into something you might see on a postcard, but there's an insider's story behind how it arrived on the property. "This fountain was the first pool in Houston County," Heather says. "Dr. Hodge would let the Baptist church come in and do baptisms."

If you want a wonderful getaway, check out Henderson Village and tell your friends, but, on the other hand, maybe we should keep it a secret just between the locals!

Directions: From Macon, head south on I-75 to exit 127. Take a right off the ramp and head on down the road about a mile. You'll see the entrance for Henderson Village on the right.

Phone: (478) 988-8696

Website: www.hendersonvillage.com

Prices: To spend the night, the rates run between $175 to $350 a night. They do have midweek and off-season specials, some for as little as $99 a night. Fishing on the property at the stocked pond full of catfish and bass is free, but hunting does come with trophy fees. Plus, you do get complimentary breakfast with one night's lodging.

Extras: Even if you don't spend the night, Henderson does have several special events during the year, including the Twelve Days of Christmas. At that time, you can have brunch with Santa and sit down for a Teddy Bear Tea.

Henderson Village also has two handicapped accessible rooms, and—this is really a bonus—they allow pets in the tenant cottages and there isn't even a weight limit on your animal. If Henderson Village doesn't have room in the cottages, you can still bring your cat or dog but they will ask you to sign a pet waiver to stay in one of the other houses. And last but not least, if you're going to the Langston House to eat, make sure to call ahead; reservations are recommended but not required. Heather says a phone call helps to make sure they're not having a wedding reception or party.

Feel free to stop in when the sign says "open".

Lane and one of his signature trays.

Pottery Studio

Along US Highway 441 in Dublin, you'll find a simple sign that says "Pottery Studio" sitting next to a humble cabin off the road. That's where the simplicity ends. Once you walk through the door, you'll see some of the most colorful pottery pieces in Central Georgia, all handmade by a guy named Lane Pollack.

Lane's mother-in-law Kay Wayne got the business up and going. The family converted an old turpentine still into a studio. As a matter of fact, the building is pretty historic, so the family has left the windows intact so you can imagine people walking up to the counter in the late 1800s.

Kay Wayne fired up her kilns in 1999. She sold all kinds of decorative and functional pieces, but one line seemed to keep going out the door. "The blue and green sold the most," Lane says. "It seemed to go with a lot of things." Those beautiful blue and green trays are the mainstay of the business. Kay did put imprints on the clay. She mostly walked out the back door and gathered up some needles off the endless supply of Mount Vernon long needle pine trees that stand so thickly in Central Georgia. She would imprint the impression of a nice sprig right in the middle of her tranquil trays.

And, besides selling like hotcakes, they caught the attention of a very special visitor. "Well, a lady from *Southern Living* stopped in the shop and saw the pine needles," Lane explains. "She took a couple of trays with her." That lady called back and said that the Southern magazine wanted to sell those trays in their catalog of cool Southern finds. Kay thought that was great until *Southern Living* told her how many they needed. "They said they needed five to seven thousand a month," Lane says, chuckling. "Mom said, '*What?*' And then she sold the rights."

Not only was Kay not ready for mass production, she wanted more time to play with the grandkids. That's when she looked to her son-in-law with an art degree from Penn State to take over the business. "Mom gave me a lump of clay and said, 'Let's see what you can do,'" Lane recalls. This then-construction worker must have done pretty well because one day Lane got a call from Kay: "She said, 'What are you doing on Tuesday because I'm going to retire and it's all yours.'"

He took it over gladly and loves working in the studio and entertaining the folks that stop in. When I came by, Lane was polishing hedgehogs and little critters that some Southwest Laurens second graders had concocted. "We give tours anytime of the day I'm here," he says. "On average, two people stop by a week and want to see everything and then they bring their church groups."

Lane is a big, easygoing guy who will walk you through the little building showing you how he molds the clay or the three big kilns that work practically twenty-four hours a day to get all the work done. He's also left his own imprint on the business. You'll still see those wonderful blue and green trays with the pine needles, but now you can also buy them with lighthouse imprints in the middle. Lane says folks like to get the Georgia ones from Tybee and St. Simon's. You can also buy everything from flower vases to sushi sets, all done in the wonderful glazes. Lane's likes to make bird and bat houses and his family has all gotten in on the act, too. In fact, just inside the door you'll discover a table full of finds made by his eight- and twelve-year-old little girls.

Lane figures one day he'll be able to push a pile of clay their way and say, "Let's see whatcha got," and the business will mold itself into the next generation.

Directions: From Macon take I-16 towards Savannah. Take exit 51 and a right off the ramp. Go about twelve and a half miles up the road. You'll see the cabin and the sign on the right side of the road.

Hours: There is nothing set in stone (only clay) here, but during the summertime he's open during daylight hours. And to put it more simply, whenever the sign outside says open, feel free to walk on in.

Phone: (478) 984-5299

Prices: Pieces range from five dollars to much higher for commissioned work. You can buy his popular trays with the lighthouses and leaves, which run twenty dollars.

Extras: If you don't want to go to Dublin to visit Lane, he does do twenty or thirty art shows a year, including Christmas Made in the South. The trays and all the pottery are fully functional so you can put any of them in the microwave and the dishwasher!

People

Some unique items at Ruel's Fourth of July sale.

*There aren't too many places you can buy an outhouse
in Central Georgia, but Ruel has two.*

Ruel Pitts

I gotta say Ruel Pitts reminds me of my Dad. Both are easygoing with a quick smile and both guys have a good bit of pack rat in them! But in Ruel's case, his hobbies outstretched my Dad's habits by a very long country mile. You see, the recently retired country boy with the overalls and floppy fishing hat sees things in a different light. What you and I may call junk, Ruel calls opportunity.

Every Fourth of July, Ruel rolls out tons of stuff for his annual garage sale. But let's be real, it's so much stuff it would take a garage the size of a football field to fit inside. Luckily, the guys got some land. And as you drive by on Highway 74, you can't miss it!

The holiday we stopped by, Ruel had a full open trailer of old soda bottles, including Coke, RC, Red Rock, and more—some of them dated back a ways. He has a lot of random stuff like car parts, vintage soda signs, and tools. One lady picked up a showerhead and asked, "Does it work?" Ruel replied, "I haven't used it myself, but I know it works and you can have it for fifty cents." He tried to make another unusual sale. "Would you be interested in a coffin for your dog?" he asked an unsuspecting browser. "Just happen to have one for you for $325. There's one for five hundred that's velvet-lined."

Such is the life of this quirky collector. I asked him where he got his giant bucket of keys. At first he said he didn't have any idea, but he got to thinking and it all came back: "A hardware store closed down on Houston Avenue. I asked him how much for all the keys. He said five dollars!"

"Ruel can tell you where he got everything," says Dianne Pitts, and she should know. She's been married to Ruel for forty-one years and put down the junk ground rules early on. "He doesn't leave it in my eyesight or he knows I'll move it. The only thing I didn't like was the school bus." You heard right; the 1959 school bus came into their lives a while back. "I bought it from my uncle and she pitched a fit," says Ruel. Deep down he understood, but he also saw the bright yellow wheels as the perfect place to store some of his loot, so they reached a compromise.

Ruel's property almost resembles a very tasteful reproduction of a small town. He's got a garage with a 1956 Chevy parked inside and a small store where folks can visit and see his really cool vintage stuff. So he made the bus fit his surroundings: "Well, I got some two-by-fours, built a frame around it, and painted it to look like a filling station." And somehow it really does all work.

You get the feeling that for Ruel a close second to collecting stuff is talking and visiting. And a good bit of that goes on right next to the filling station at the store. It's amazing to walk inside this pop culture museum. As Ruel offers you a cold Coca-Cola from the bottle, he'll tell you stories of how he collected the California Raisins, all the Texaco memorabilia, and the Radio Flyer replicas. You'll also see a giant Keebler elf head, a collection of Master locks, Tom's Chips canisters, and Prince Albert in a can. This is a special place with stuff close to Ruel's heart. "Every now and then, he'll sell out of the store," explains Dianne, "and I'll say, 'Honey, you don't want to do that.'" Dianne's just playing the protector. All of the stuff inside these walls came from family, like her mom's spelling book that dates back to 1908 or the 2-liter, glass Coca Cola bottles a Mrs. McGhee gave Ruel years ago.

But don't worry, you can treasure all the things from the past, but Ruel has plenty of the unusual for you to walk away with— like the world's largest salt and pepper shakers that double as bathrooms! Ruel even had his shakers on eBay. He got a lot of hits, but no one actually bought the brightly painted Port-O-Lets with Sky Chief and Texaco signs on top. "Actually, I've decided I'm not going to sell those," he says.

I'm glad. It's nice to know you can always stop by and get a real history lesson, and yet discover stuff with the kind of touch only a Ruel Pitts can put on life.

Directions: From Macon, take Mercer University Drive west out of town. Mercer runs into Highway 74. Ruel's place is right at mile marker 11, 15 miles past I-475.

Hours/Seasons: The big Fourth of July sale lasts about a week. Ruel says you can stop by anytime though for a tour or a little shopping.

Phone: (478) 994-5952

Extras: At the sale you can buy stuff for a nickel all the way up to hundreds of dollars.

Mark's pieces come to life outdoors.

Mark Smith

Mark Smith is a guy who you might call a true mountain man. When most folks walk through the woods they appreciate the scenery, but this self-described craftsman sees opportunity. "Yeah. I look at the trees and say, 'Oh, I could do something with that.'"

Not just any old something, Mark has a special talent to shape wood to create beautiful pieces of art and functional furniture. But I might be getting a little ahead of myself because when I met Mark one fall afternoon and talked on the back of his porch, he shared a history that's as fascinating as his handiwork.

Mark joined the army in 1985 and served as a chopper pilot in the Persian Gulf War as a chief warrant officer. "I always thought pilots were guys like John Wayne and Tom Cruise. Then you add Mark Smith. Ain't nothin' to it," he says with a humble grin.

When he got back, things didn't click right away. He was going through a divorce and his job as a school teacher just wasn't working out. Then he met a woman named Lila. "I was homeless at the time—not living under a bridge homeless—I was living in a deer camp." They went to a NASCAR race and when they got back Mark spoke those words every woman wants to hear at the end of a date: "You want to go talk to the cows?" You gotta think it's that boyishness mixed with the spirit of a true Southern gentleman that won her over, but actually Mark's carpentry skills sealed the deal. Lila owned a beautiful unfinished mountain home in Jones County. "We always say I needed a place to live and she needed a carpenter to finish the house," Mark says.

He's still not done with the house, but when you walk inside it's easy to see where his skills really began to take off. The cavernous cabin is lined with huge trunks of trees serving as ornate banisters. But as Mark worked on the house, a transition came: "I was beating up wood, just making stuff for the house. I didn't know it was folk art."

But Lila did. She convinced Mark to take some of his pieces to Payne City (an antique warehouse). "Payne City turned it down and I said, 'See, Lila. Nobody likes my stuff except you and you're being nice,'" Mark explains. He's quick to jump the gun because the folks at Payne City just said, "Hey, we're antiques. This belongs across the street at the Middle Georgia Art Association."

That all happened a few years ago, and now Mark has quite a reputation. He creates chairs, benches, beds, and even candle-holders and vases. His porch is a holding area for various pieces of wood. Everything from shavings to gigantic trunks sit around waiting for Mark's brain to give them a permanent place in the world. It's a process that takes some time. "I looked at my first table three years before I knew what to do with it. I call it Monkey Dust. Every piece I make just has to speak to me."

Nowadays, it doesn't take three years for the wood to start talking, but everything that Mark makes does hold a little piece of his heart. As you might have guessed, he names each item. He has a table called Forgotten Soldiers in honor of his army friends that never came home, and another table named No Wake. It resembles a manatee, which makes sense since the ocean is another passion in his life.

If you buy a piece of Marks work, treasure it: "If you're not going to keep it inside and protect it, I'm not going to sell it to you," he says matter of factly. It's the only thing he's adamant about because when a veteran puts his soul into a piece of wood, you just don't want to see it ruined.

Phone: (478) 986-5296. You can call for an appointment to come out to the house or have Mark come to yours.

Website: www.no2alike.biz

Extras: Mark's work is in various shops around Central Georgia, including Sparkle Plenty in Madison.

Salty's Excellent Adventure

For this next adventure, I needed a little help. You see Tyler's Place is a dog park, so I figured who best to tell you first hand what it's all about than our dog Salty. Salty is a rambunctious, energetic, sweet Australian Shepherd, and he does have some great social skills. So I turned over the pen, paper, and laptop to him. You may want to call your dog over to the book while you read about it and then both of you can load up and head to the dog park!

—Suzanne

Salty and Tyler got pretty tired playing all afternoon.

Tyler's a happy dog whenever he gets to romp at the Macon Dog Park.

Tyler's Place

Every morning, I get up ready and raring to go. After all, I am a dog and one of the best things in life is running and sniffing in wide-open spaces. On very special days, Suzanne and I jump in the truck and head to Tyler's Place. Taking a trip here is better than a pile of Milk Bones.

It's a fenced-in field, about 4 or 5 acres with a stream running right down the middle, which makes it nice to cool off my paws when I run around so much. They also have a few fire hydrants and you know us dogs love those. Plus, there are plenty of places for the humans to sit and talk with each other while us dogs romp through the grass.

Betty Lou Brown sits on the board of Historic Macon. She told me this wonderful ground sat empty and fenced up for quite sometime. The city took a closer look at the property when the area went through neighborhood revitalization (That's a big word for a dog.). At the same time, Betty Lou's son visited a dog park in Athens and told her Macon needed the same thing. "Well, the land seemed perfect," she says, "so a group organized to form the dog park. We had no money at all but we made a list."

The city got on board and brought in mowers to knock down the giant weeds and the project started to come together. In October 2004, the first dogs romped around on the grass.

About the same time another situation was developing. Reva Ann Dame loved animals, and when she found out she had a terminal disease she made a list of charities to receive money from her estate. She had to look no further than into the sweet eyes of her constant companion Tyler to know that the dog park would make the list. She allotted $76,000 to go to the project after her death. Dame said, "Somehow we take care of people but we don't always take care of animals."

"You can't believe how happy we were to get the money," Betty says. The dog park group replaced the chain link fence with a pretty iron setup and they planted lots of trees. And, thanks to Reva Ann, there is also a cool water fountain where dogs and humans can get a drink. And I gotta tell you, after running around with my friends for an hour or so, a dog needs a big drink!

And as for Tyler, well don't you worry one bit about him. As you can see by the pictures, we had a great time together that afternoon. A friend of the family is taking good care of him; he even has two kids to play with and a cat to chase around. I barked a question to Reva Ann's friend Madge Knott. I asked her if she thought Reva Anne would be proud looking down. Madge said, "I think she would be happy. She was such a generous person. She wanted to do something that would make a difference."

Betty Lou says the place does make a big difference; she figures about a 100 dogs bring their owners in for a little fun every week! "I think the dogs love it," she said. "They love to run and chase and smell and then they go home very tired."

I gotta say I'm tired right now after all of this typing. No wonder dogs don't write books, but make sure you take your best friend to the Macon Dog Park. Take a frisbee or a tennis ball, too. Both of you are sure to have a tail wagging good time. See ya there.

—Salty

Directions: The park is located near Mercer University, one block north of Tattnall Square at the corner of Chestnut and Adams streets. From I-75, take exit 164 and head east towards downtown on Hardeman. At the first light, take a right onto Monroe. This street becomes Tattnall when you pass under the railroad bridge. Turn right again onto Chestnut Street and look for the park on the right after you cross Adams Street.

Phone: (478) 751-9280

Website: www.macondogpark.org

Prices: Tyler's Place is completely free, but you can join the Friends of the Dog Park if you would like to make a donation. They also have volunteer cleanup days if you would like to help out.

Extras: The park does have some basic rules for canines and their companions.

A. Dogs must come in with basic good manners.

B. All dogs must have current rabies shots and vaccines.

C. Each person can only have three dogs in the park at one time.

D. Dog owners must be present with their canines.

Some people have organized breed days where they meet up and socialize to exchange information. The park is certainly open to everyone else on those days; it's just a little something extra. Sniff out the website for the latest information.

And one last thing: if you have a small dog and you're worried about it running around with the big dogs like me, don't worry. The dog park has a partitioned off an area just for small dogs.

Thanks for reading
More Cotton, Cornbread, and Conversations.
I hope it leads you to new adventures.
If you come across a new adventure, contact me.
It may wind up in our next book!

Suzanne Lawler
^{c}/o Mercer University Press
1400 Coleman Avenue
Macon GA 31207